Learning to Do Your Very Best: 6 Habits for Academic Success

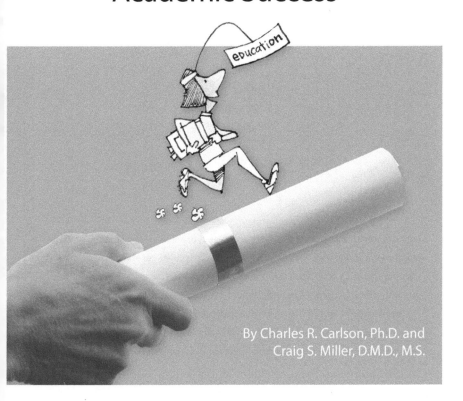

By Charles R. Carlson, Ph.D. and
Craig S. Miller, D.M.D., M.S.

ISBN: 978-1-477-67041-5

Publisher:

Summer Workshop

5026 Ashgrove Road

Nicholasville, KY 40356

Graphic Designer: Sheri Wood, The Arion Group

Illustrators: Chris Ware, Matt Hazard

Dedication

We dedicate this book to Dr. Mark V. Thomas,
dedicated academician, who always encouraged
students to "drink from the fountain of knowledge."

Our Thank You

This book is written for all the students who need help in achieving their academic success, and all those who have achieved that success and shared their stories with us.

We thank **Cindy** and **Sherry** our wives and best friends for always supporting us, and our children **Jeremiah, Susan, Bethany, Cameron** and **Samuel** for enduring the love and direction provided by your parents.

We thank **C. Rodney Scott** for introducing us to several of these concepts and how learning skills can change a person's trajectory.

Thanks are also offered to **Chris Ware** and **Matt Hazard** our illustrators, **Sheri Wood** our graphic designer, **Richard Smith** for review and offering editorial advice, and **Tom Pabin** for supporting the concept of learning as it relates to the college planning process.

Table of Contents

Preface

One of the greatest gifts in life is to impart knowledge, wisdom and happiness to others. This transfer of knowledge is a key ingredient to improving friendships, families and society that hopefully will bring lives of peace and prosperity to future generations.

Every year we see bright students underperform in school – whether it is high school, or college, and even at graduate and professional level courses. And you too, probably have observed students who are successful academically and others who are not. These observations led us to wonder:

"Why is this occurring?

Why isn't someone doing something about it?

And, what can we do to help?"

The Problem: Underperformance. *Many high schools and colleges graduate only about 70% of their students. Even the best colleges graduate about 90% of their students.* And, although 10% to 30% of students are not graduated, an even higher percentage are underperforming. Student underperformance occurs for a variety of reasons and rarely is there just one cause that stands behind disappointing academic achievement. Difficulties often arise from students entering a new and more complicated environment, and teachers expecting students to know how to study and perform well on assignments, quizzes and exams. For students, the material is often more complicated, more time consuming and may not come to them naturally. Also, tests often come in groups of two or three at a time and cause great difficulty for some students. For teachers, there is an expectation that students already have learned how to study during their formative years (i.e., Grades 1 through 8). Thus, teachers assume that you are an effective learner by the time you reach high school. High school teachers and college professors, in turn, often view their jobs as communicators of information. These teachers are focused on being responsible for teaching the material and what students need to learn, **not on *how* you go about learning**. This mindset has led to a gap in thought between '**learning**' and '**how do I learn?**' In this book, we focus on "HOW DO I LEARN?" by providing you with a number of specific habits and strategies that will lead to your academic success.

Why is this important? Learning "how to learn" (or study) is one of the most important tasks you need for success in academics and life. It is the combined use of planning, time-management, organization, effort and practice in the skills of thinking, observing, concentrating, and analyzing information. The end result is the grade you earn and the opportunities you are offered, in the future, based on your current academic performance.

Why hasn't someone done something about it? Actually, many people have done something about it. There are orientation sessions on studying, tutors at most schools, and learning centers dedicated to helping students learn. Additionally, online resources and many books on the topic are available.[1-12] Many of these resources are excellent for describing how to read, write, learn and take tests effectively. However, most students are seldom introduced to these resources. And, seldom is there a separate course dedicated to the "how to's." That is, how to learn, how to study, how to complete assignments and how to perform well on exams. The students that have been introduced to these resources and discovered the important aspects of learning, time management, memorization and test-taking have clearly benefitted. And, their scholarly achievement and the rewards that accompany academic success are a testament to the value of these skills.

How can we help? We decided at the beginning of this writing that students would benefit from a course and book dedicated to instilling habits for academic success. We decided to provide clear, simple and direct advice that would *greatly favor* academic success. We have been helping students individually since we both became teachers over 20 years ago. We have interviewed students at all levels extensively and spent hours with graduate and professional students in one-on-one tutoring. Most strikingly from these experiences, was the common theme that academically successful students implemented study strategies that were different and *more efficient* than those students who were struggling academically.

In this book we provide you with these methods. The methods are simple and easy to learn, and target your behavior, your brain and your thinking. The study habits we present will help you reach your academic potential by teaching you how to gain knowledge, how to use knowledge and how to demonstrate mastery of that knowledge. Each chapter contains "quotes" from the authors that focus you to the important information, and each chapter is purposely short in length so you can learn new methods quickly and use your time efficiently — this book can likely be read in a few hours. Chapters are also written in a manner that addresses things you should do sequentially to achieve your academic success. They include how to:

1) know what you want
2) grasp new information
3) organize and be time efficient
4) prepare for exams
5) take tests well, and
6) be a balanced person.

A common theme in academics is that every student is different and every student studies differently. **However, most academically successful students have similar habits that target them for success and don't take much time.** This book targets those techniques. This book is for all students who want to perform better, who are not achieving the grades they really want, and for students who want an efficient method for learning.

Wishing you all the best in all your (academic) pursuits!

Charley Craig

Target what you want.

In this chapter you will learn the importance of:

1) Motivation
2) Education
3) Setting goals
4) Investing in yourself
5) The rewards of having a good education

Aprille, a high school junior, just got her exam back. It wasn't a terrible shock that she received a 66%. She hadn't studied much, instead she had spent most of the night before the exam texting one of her friends, Tamatha, who also received a 66%. Aprille was doing okay in her other classes and was satisfied with her performance. "After all, I really don't care much about school" she tells her friends all the time. One of her other friends, Tom, realizes that Aprille could do better. He said that she rarely does homework or studies, she only wants to get by with the least amount of effort, and rarely follows the guidelines provided by the teacher. Her motivation for doing well in school is lacking, mostly from living in the moment. Let's look at what it takes to fix this, as this is a key first step to academic success.

Getting there by knowing the value of motivation, identifying your goals, and investing in yourself.

It may be difficult for you to realize it, but education is important. You hear your parents tell you this, you hear your teachers tell you this, but for some reason it takes a while for it to sink in. Your parents, teachers and advisors tell you that getting an education leads to knowledge and understanding, and that education helps you get a good job that improves your chances for success in the future. And, they are right. However, education is so much more.

Education is a chance to learn and become informed. It is a chance to interact with teachers, and socialize with your friends and make new friends. It is a chance to exercise your brain and see how you perform in unique environments and under different kinds of pressure. It is the chance to listen, read, and formulate your own thoughts, develop new skills and apply new principles. Education is learning. It transforms you with new knowledge, thoughts and abilities that will allow you to do new things, go new places, and be a better and more civic-minded person. Education will allow you to consider new ideas, new things, and the diversity of the world.

Yes, education is important, but **realizing** this is even more important. This realization is the first step in doing well in school and society. Education is important because it leads to intelligent thought and better decisions. It expands your mind and makes it more adaptable to change, when there are reasons to do so. Learning information also bit by bit, provides the framework for additional learning. The incremental learning process allows your brain to gather information more efficiently, and develop an understanding of information. Thus as your memory grows, you assess the pros and cons of situations better, that, in turn, guides you towards improvements in your life and the lives of others.

> ## "Education is important, but realizing that is even more important."

1. Get motivated. To do well in academics you need to be motivated to do so. In contrast, lack of motivation is the best way to do poorly in school, college and life in general. In fact, if you are not motivated, even the best study habits and test taking skills are unlikely to help you do well in school.

Motivation – a noun meaning: that desire to do something well – is the key to excellent academic performance. In your case, you should be motivated to learn and achieve because there are many benefits for doing so. For the "A" student, motivation is often already in place. They are ambitious, and they have already set a goal of being academically successful and may already have a career path outlined for themselves (e.g., "I want to be a pharmacist"). However, many students have not set a goal and are unclear of their future. For those unclear of their goals, it is reasonable for you to ask "how will I do well, if I don't have the will to do well?"

> ## "Motivation is the key to excellent academic performance."

At the heart of the matter for some students is the question, "Why should I be academically ambitious? What's in it for me?" The answer is "being motivated and ambitious for knowledge leads to many rewards including: good grades, personal growth and satisfaction, self-confidence, self-improvement, and better self-control." These qualities bring about kindness, creativity and strength, and the willingness to help others and society. This, in turn, leads to improvements in your friendships, family and love life, finances, and society.

"Education leads to many rewards."

Some students are indifferent, and haven't really thought much about academic performance. They live in the moment and haven't yet looked themselves in a mirror and asked "what do I really want in my life and what do I really want from leading my life?" For these students, we encourage a few quiet moments of introspection, thinking of these things, then setting some personal goals. Setting personal goals for achievement are your key motivators. Without goals, there is often no direction and drive to achieve.

2. Set clear goals. So, the second secret to academic success is to establish clear goals for academic performance. This is important because **you will likely achieve only the goals that you set.** Interestingly, one of the best predictors of classroom performance is obtained by asking, "what is the lowest grade in this course that I can achieve and still be personally satisfied?" Yes, satisfied. Will your answer be an "A", "B", "C" or "D." The choice of an "A" or "B" reflects academic ambition, whereas the choice of "C" or lower reflects indifference towards your academic performance.

Remember, the foundation for your academic performance is based on your level of motivation and ambition. And, ambition can be influenced or undermined by many factors including your health and well being, friends and family (social influences) and economic matters. For example, your ambitions can easily be frustrated by a parental breakup, lack of money to buy food or clothes, or a job that limits your ability to study in the evening. And, you can be tugged daily by these external and internal factors which will at times make it difficult for you to remember to "Put Studying High on Your Priorities – and in many cases as your FIRST PRIORITY."

"Set a goal that studying and learning are high priorities."

In Arthur Kornhauser's book, "How to Study" he emphasized that a 'driving motive' is a key fundamental requirement for effective study, and we could not agree more. Motivation is key to your success. Thus, it is critical for you to take a moment to look inside and ask yourself, "DO I WANT ACADEMIC SUCCESS?" For many, the answer is clear as these students have a short- and long-term plan for college and their career afterwards. These students can look into the future and know that good academic performance is critical for their long-term plans. However, for many students this question has not been asked, nor thoughtfully considered, and can be complicated by the fact that they don't know what future path they should take.

"You achieve only the goals that you set."

Thinking about your level of motivation. A method for addressing your LEVEL OF MOTIVATION follows. First, we encourage you to find a quiet place to think about the question of academic success and what level you wish to achieve. We recommend picking a spot under a tree or in a comfortable quiet room with plenty of windows where you can absorb the beauty of nature on a nice day away from a lot of people, noise and distractions. Close your eyes and picture the future following academic successes, that is being graduated from high school or college with an "A" grade point average - *Take the moment now and close your eyes. Keep them closed for about a minute while you think about your future.*

Now, picture the opposite - the outcomes associated with academic mediocrity or failure. Think about the different social, financial, health and leisure activities associated with successful outcomes versus failing outcomes.

Conjure up images about your friends, family and loved ones who will share your successes and failures and choose where you want to be. Make your decision today. And, at the end of this exercise, the answer to this simple question should be – *I want to do my best, I want success in learning, and I want to have fun while doing it.*

3. <u>Set goals early</u>. Whatever you choose to do in life, we believe you want to be a successful learner, so regardless of what life brings your way, you can adapt and achieve success. The establishment of clear goals focuses your attention and helps you identify how best to spend your time and personal resources.

At the earliest possible moment in your academic life, you need to implement a strategy for success. At the beginning of each academic semester, think about the grade point average you want for that semester. That is, what is the lowest grade you would be satisfied earning (for each class) and still be satisfied and happy with yourself. Then, write it down for each class. Put your goals for academic performance in a visible place on your wall, bulletin board or screen-saver of your computer, phone or day-timer so you can see your goals frequently. Revisit your goals when things get tough and when you have doubts. Use your goals to focus mentally, to help re-energize yourself, and use your motivation to begin the process of positive thinking towards achieving academic success.

"Write down your goals for each class."

4. Invest in Yourself. Education is an investment. So is eating right, getting enough sleep and exercise and having happiness in your life. All these things are investments in you. And, like most investments there is a return on your investment. In this case, the immediate return is learning and the good grades that result will increase your opportunities for good health and well-being.

Now you may or may not have thought that education is an investment, however getting an education costs time and money. In fact, there is a cost in acquiring most knowledge. Public elementary and high school education costs your parents money through their tax dollars. Private education costs tuition dollars. This cost is often paid for by parents, grandparents or loved ones. At the University level, courses cost between $200 and $1000 per credit hour. Which means you (or your parents) are paying the college instructor to teach you at a rate that is many times more than the rate it costs to get other services, such as food from a restaurant, automotive repair and other labor intensive services. So, spend your money and time wisely.

"Your education is an investment. Treat it as your most important investment."

One of the best predictors of good academic performance is your self-investment in the process. You can be invested either *emotionally* (i.e., being motivated) or *financially* (i.e., by paying for a part or all of your education in one way or another…sometimes students take scholarships where they know they will have to perform public service after their education) or both. We have found, the best student academic performers are invested in both. These students are focused on academics, realize the importance of good grades, and get their work done quickly and on time.

Time and time again, we have seen students who are **not** invested *emotionally* and *financially* perform poorly. These students lack motivation and a strategy for academic success. They don't have a plan and don't care about their performance. They haven't looked into the future or thought about who they want to be and what they have to do to get there. They are not paying for their education, so the cost is not apparent or important, yet. However, it is after the first set of poor grades or the end of the semester when they begin to realize their predicament. This in turn leads to emotional stress, and tension between the student and whoever might be paying the tuition.

me anD You,
BuDDY... We'Re
GoinG pLaces!

So, let's get off onto the right footing and increase your chances of doing well in school. The best way to do this is to invest in your education. If you are in college, pay for some or all of your tuition. This can be direct dollars from your savings, a scholarship you receive, or a loan you need to repay. By investing your own money or other self-generated income/service, you realize the value of your educational investment and you are more likely to be motivated. At the high school level, you don't need to invest your money yet, but realize the time is coming for you to do so when you enter college.

> Time and time again, we have seen students who are not invested emotionally and financially perform poorly.

Your investment is your motivation, time and energy. In fact, this goes for all students at the high school and college level. **Be motivated, set goals and invest time in your academics.**

"Provide your educational investment with the proper amount of motivation, time, energy and finances, as possible."

THiS won't take LonG!

Here are some facts regarding the benefits of education and the associated costs and investments.

- **Education creates economic growth by 1) creating new knowledge and 2) transmitting that knowledge. In turn, education increases productivity, technology and wealth.**

- **Educated workers have advantages relative to less-educated workers including higher wages, greater employment stability, and greater upward mobility in income.**

- **Education improves your opportunity for finding and getting the job you want.** In today's world getting a good job is not as easy as in the decades before. Three factors are largely influencing the need for jobs and the economic landscape. These include 1) the global economy, 2) use of, and rapid change in, technology, and 3) rising customer expectations – that is a smarter consumer. Education prepares you for these demands.

- **The amount of education directly influences the quality of employment.** By the time you complete 4 years of college education, you will likely invest between $20,000 and $200,000 in your education. The return on this investment is generally between 3 to 10X more annual pay than non-college educated laborers. This translates to greater than $1 million dollars more over your lifetime compared to the average non-college educated laborer.

Specifically, the average baccalaureate will earn $20,000 more annually than the average high school graduate. The average master's degree recipient will earn $24,000 more annually than the average high school graduate. And, the average professional (doctoral level training, e.g., Ph.D., D.M.D., M.D or Pharm.D.) will earn about $70,000 more annually than the average high school graduate.

• **Education teaches you to be a life-long learner that will help you upgrade your skills continuously and improve your overall performance.**

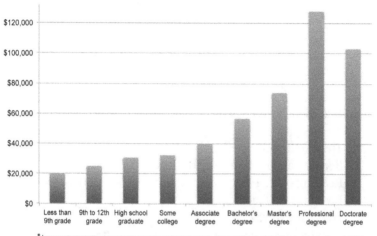

Mean Earning of All Full-Time Workers, by Educational Attainment: 2009*

* Income estimates in this table are based on money earnings before taxes. The population all persons 25 years and over, who worked full-time all year in 2009. Adapted from U.S. Census Bureau. The 2012 Statistical Abstract: The National Data Book, Table P-232. http://www.census.gov/compendia/statab/cats/education/educational_attainment.html

Summary Habit 1:

• Realize that education is an important investment.

• Establish your goals for academic achievement at the beginning.

• Be a regular contributor to the process by regularly attending class, doing the reading assignments and studying well in advance of the exams. In return, your investment will pay dividends.

Grasp new information.

Get it right from the textbook and in-class

In this chapter you will learn the importance of:

1) The SQ3R method
2) Reading assignments before class
3) Reading course material in designated 30 minute blocks
4) Being time efficient
5) Using key words
6) Good note taking
7) Visiting with the instructor.

ALEX'S CASE

Alex, a freshman, came with a dream of doing well in school so he could achieve his goal of becoming a health professional. Unfortunately, that was not happening in his basic sciences and math classes even though he was taking the typical freshman load (general chemistry, math, biology, English composition, and psychology for a total of 16 hours). In fact, he had recently been encouraged by one of his science professors to choose another career path, because he hadn't demonstrated the abilities necessary to do well in college-level work. When he walked into my office, he was dejected and discouraged. After a few minutes of conversation, it became clear that the problem was not a lack of motivation or ability, but rather, he had not been trained to be a good student; he really didn't know how to study and learn efficiently. His primary strategy for studying was re-reading his textbooks and class notes two to three times before a test. However, this is not the best method for learning. Once we introduced him to specific study skills that included how to learn from textbooks, how to organize a professor's lecture and take good notes, and how to prepare for tests, he came back beaming, because of the dramatic improvement in his grades.

1. **Succeed by learning.** Academic success is linked to establishing habits that lead to effective learning. This chapter is about developing the habit of efficiently learning new information.

People learn in three ways. First, through transfer of information. This can occur by **reading, listening** and/or **observing**. Second, we l**earn from making mistakes** and realizing that a method, or way of doing something, doesn't work. Third, we can learn from other's mistakes – either by observation, listening or reading. We begin this chapter with an effective method for learning information from reading.

Learning from the Written Word: The SQ3R Method

There are number of approaches to learning new information, particularly when that information comes from books. Perhaps the single most powerful method developed to date is called the SQ3R approach. Mastery of this five-step approach to learning new information can improve your study efficiency and maximize remembering that information for tests.

2. Survey before you read. The first step in the SQ3R process is to survey a section of the material to be read before the reading begins. The purpose of the survey is to see what to expect from your reading and to develop questions about what you will read. This usually means focusing first on about five to seven pages of a chapter in a standard text and not the whole chapter. When you try to survey too much material it becomes difficult to manage the amount of information. It's OK to scan the overall assignment so that you grasp the total volume of material and can begin planning how much time you'll need to devote to your reading and studying. However, a survey should focus on a more manageable length of *five-to-seven* pages starting with the beginning of the assignment.

> SQ3R Method
>
> • Survey/Skim
>
> • Question
>
> • 3R - Read
>   Recite
>   Review

"Survey five-to-seven pages of the reading."

In doing a survey, quickly skim over the first five-to-seven page section of the reading assignment and notice any titles, main headings, pictures, summaries, and graphs that make up the format of many textbooks in use today. When you have essays, short stories and novel-length books, the survey can still be used, but titles and first lines of paragraphs become much more important. Typi-

cally, important ideas are conveyed in the titles, topic headings, pictures, summaries, and graphs. We also encourage students to read the FIRST SENTENCE of several paragraphs and the CONCLUDING PAGE– since the conclusion directs the reader to the important information in the chapter. The survey provides an overall picture of what will be covered in the reading.

It is reported that students read faster after they survey what they are about to read. Just like it is common to drive faster on more familiar roads, you generally read faster when there is an awareness of what is coming. Remember that the *survey* should take only a couple of minutes and prepare you to ask questions that the reading will answer.

3. Ask questions, and write them down. Based on the survey, the second step in the SQ3R approach is to ask *questions* that could be answered from the material that will be read. This typically means two to three questions should be developed from the survey, but this number may vary depending on the difficulty of the material. Then, either write the questions in a notebook or ask them out loud to yourself. Writing them down in a special notebook used for the purpose of studying material for an individual class, or asking them out loud helps prevent a student from lying to her/himself – believing they know something when they don't. The habit of writing something down or saying something out loud is a good way of minimizing the likelihood that you will be lying to yourself. Writing down questions also provides a ready resource, or study guide, that can be used during your review for the examination.

> "One of the greatest pitfalls to learning is telling yourself that you know something when you really don't."

4. Read in 5 to 7 page blocks. Step three in the SQ3R process is to read the *five-to-seven* page section that you have just surveyed. Yes, you want to read chapters in five to seven page blocks. The reading should be done with a focus on answering the questions you have posed. It is good to underline or highlight key ideas that answer the questions when reading, but be careful not to overuse this strategy. Underlining or highlighting material provides a good way of drawing attention to important ideas for reviewing later. However, don't over do it. Underlining too much can be distracting and can detract from finding the most important information.

> "Read five to seven pages, underline or highlight as you go."

5. Recite the answers. After reading and highlighting, you should turn your attention to the second "r", *recite*. In this step you should recite answers to questions developed from the survey. It is very important to answer these questions out loud. Answering the questions out loud is an efficient way to find out what has been learned. Taking the time to write out answers to questions is not very efficient and is generally too time-consuming, unless you use only short phrases. Reciting the answers to questions out loud is better. It helps ensure

that you 'know the answer to that' and helps avoid fooling yourself of material you think you know, but really don't know. Saying the answer out loud, while looking away from the text, helps ensure that an idea is clearly developed. If an answer to a question is not known, don't worry about it, but mark/highlight it and come back to it after all the other questions are completed. In this way, your time for studying is managed most efficiently, and the material you don't know has been clearly marked.

"Recite answers to your questions out loud."

One of the key points of this book is to help develop efficient study habits. Determining what you don't know, and focusing your studying on those things that you don't know is one of the most important concepts for effective study and prepares you for the final step in the SQ3R method, *review*.

"During your reciting, identify the questions to which you don't know the answer. Mark or highlight these questions."

6. Review. The review process involves periodically going back to the questions developed in the survey and answering them out loud. If you do not know the answer, re-read only those paragraphs that allow you to answer that question. Stay focused here, and don't read many pages; just focus on the paragraphs that will answer the question. Then move on to the next question on the list.

Be aware that short, frequent (at least weekly) reviews are far superior to long and infrequent reviews. In fact, as much as possible, try to review any new material as quickly as possible after the original learning takes place. Studies have shown that recall immediately after original learning is a very powerful way to remember information for long periods of time. Thus, a short review taking less than five minutes after a class where you recite answers to questions about the main points in a just completed lecture is one of the best investments for academic success that can be made.

"Use short reviews right after class to recite answers to questions about the main points of the lecture."

The SQ3R method is a time-tested strategy for learning new information from textbooks or any written material. Some will argue about the "extra" time this method requires. On the other hand, doing a survey alone will improve reading speed and gain valuable time back. Rereading material will increase comprehension slightly the first time. Additional rereading will help very little if at all. It is much more effective to recite and review material based on questions developed from the original survey than to spend precious time re-reading. However, there is evidence that working test-related problems as you review information will be helpful in learning that information and performing well on future tests (see Chapter 4).

7. Read assignments before class. Finally, a word about when to read. Generally, you should try to read the material related to class before the actual class sessions so that you are prepared. At the very least, however, you will want to read the material within 48 hours of when the lecture on that material was presented. This allows you to blend what you heard in class with the actual reading assignment.

"Read the material before, or within 48 hours, of the lecture."

8. Read in 30 minute blocks of time. Another thing to think about is the length of time you want to devote to reading a section of material. Our recommendation is that you plan for 30 minute reading sessions. This will enable you to focus your attention, and then take a short break. Additionally, if you put yourself under time pressure during your study time it can help you when it comes time to take tests under time pressure. You should use a timer or clock to help you become aware of the time allotted for this study activity. Research has demonstrated that mental performance is best when the conditions for performance are like the conditions when the original learning took place.

9. Learn from the lecture. Make the time in class count is another key habit for success as a student. It is surprising how many students decide that going

to class is a "waste of time." Our view is that it can be time well-spent if you are able to take advantage of that time to learn new information.

10. Use key words. One of the keys for learning new information from what you hear or read is the ability to translate what you hear or read into key words. *Key words* carry the essentials of communication and act as magnets to recall information that you have learned. For example, recall that SQ3R summarizes a significant amount of information. Similarly, each individual letter stands for a key word that also summarizes important information. Just visualizing SQ3R enables you to remember a large amount of information about how to learn in a rapid fashion. Effective use of *key words* makes the task of learning so much more efficient. Just as the use of *key words* is valuable when you are learning new information from reading, key words are essential to use when you are listening to someone present new information in a classroom.

"Translate what you hear into key words."

This section presumes that you come to a class awake, alert, and engaged. You can't do your best if you are not ready to learn. It's also not uncommon for many of us to have trouble listening after 5-10 minutes as our focus of attention drifts to other things. We have the capacity to listen at almost 800 words per minute, which is much faster than most people can speak (i.e., most speakers go at a rate of about 150 words per minute). With such a difference in comprehension ability as compared to a speaker's limited capacity to speak that fast, it is not surprising that it is pretty easy not to stay tuned to what is being said by a speaker. Therefore, you need to have a strategy for focusing your attention on what is being said if you want to avoid letting your mind wander. The strategy described below is designed to help you stay focused and learn from a speaker so that your class time is used effectively.

The first task for a student hearing information in a classroom is to *translate* what is being said into *key words*. In other words, the task is to pick out the essentials of communication from all that is heard. This process of active translation is possible because you can listen at a speed that is considerably faster than most people can speak. Rather than letting your mind wander as a speaker provides details, stories or examples to elaborate key ideas, an effective and efficient student uses the time to create "*key words*" that summarize the information being communicated and act as magnets to help in the process of recalling the information at a later date. The use of key words requires active analysis of what is being said by the teacher so that the essentials of communication can be reduced to *key words*. Since key words efficiently summarize information, they also serve as the building blocks for effective note taking. Making use of *key words* is the foundation for efficient learning while you are listening or reading. Almost everything that is heard or read can be reduced to *key words*. An effective student learns how to translate new information into *key words* quickly and efficiently.

One of the advantages of active translation of new information into *key words* is that you become an engaged learner. You are also preparing yourself for efficient and effective note taking. There are some classes where the teacher is well-organized and provides clear and concise audiovisual help for taking notes (like PowerPoint slides). Beware, however, do not become a "transcriber of words" only. It can be very easy to copy information in these classes, and to make no attempt at actively creating your own *key words* to summarize the information while busily copying information into notes. Alternatively, some instructors provide Powerpoint slides as a handout, or a downloadable file of some sort like on a Blackboard, and in these circumstances many students feel as if they don't need to take any notes. Whether you don't take any notes or you try to transcribe every word, both of these situations deprive you of active learning – the process of making your brain active during the information exchange between teacher and student. Be an active learner in the classroom.

> **"You should take advantage of classroom time to learn by actively translating information you hear into key words."**

It may also occur (quite frequently in our experience) that you'll find yourself in classes where the professor or teacher is not well organized and does not have audiovisual aids to help you learn. In these situations, it becomes essential that you "organize the teacher" so that you can learn the new information efficiently. The starting point for organizing a teacher's lecture is using key words to summarize information that is heard. Then you must figure out how the pieces of information (*key words*) fit together in an outline or diagram that you can understand and is meaningful to you. There is great value in organizing *key words* in a way that makes sense to you; after all you are the one who has to remember them. While it's true that you will want to fashion your learning after your teacher since s/he will be preparing the tests or quizzes, it is important that you use your own words and organizational approach to help you study the materials. After all, each of us learns differently, and it is important to use what works for each of us to make learning most effective and lasting.

11. Take notes using key words. Note taking is organizing key words into a meaningful structure. As main ideas are summarized into 3-5 key word phrases, these phrases are then put into relationships with other phrases using an outline format suited to the task. Most commonly, the format for expressing relationships is the standard outline using numbers and letters to identify main headings and subheadings (for example, I, II, III, A, B, C), but sometimes diagrams or charts can also be used effectively.

An outline organizes thoughts and the *key words*. The process of organizing key word information also helps in remembering that information and can reduce the need for further memorization efforts. There is a simple idea behind an outline structure. The idea is to list key words so they are organized in a way that creates relationships amongst the *key words*. This organization allows you to understand sequence and order, groups/categories, as well as similarities and differences. Often this can be done in the context of a question. For example suppose you listen to a talk where the first three *key words* you hear are people, men, and women. The organizational question, "in what way are men and women alike, yet different from people?" yields a possible organizational structure like this:

People
a. Men b. Women

This organizational structure suggests relationships and helps answer the question, "in what way are men and women alike, yet different from people?" by demonstrating that men and women are subsets of the larger category, people.

Using this basic principle, you can organize large sets of *key words* into meaningful frameworks. Interestingly, the use of this strategy also creates organizational structures that will aid in remembering the information. Also, the mental effort required to create meaningful organizational structures for yourself will help in the process of remembering this information. The use of this organizational strategy puts you in control of developing an outline that has meaning for yourself and makes you an active participant in the learning process.

12. Review immediately – the 5 minute investment. Once a lecture is over and you have completed taking your notes, you have an opportunity to take advantage of one of the most powerful tools in your learning arsenal. Remember that in our discussion of the SQ3R method we pointed out the value of immediate review of the material that was learned. Immediate review is one of the single most powerful strategies for remembering new information and it's so easy to do. You can accomplish immediate review by turning main points of the lecture into questions and seeing if you can answer those questions briefly and out loud before you leave the classroom. This exercise should take less than five minutes for you to accomplish. The rewards for these five-minute study periods will pay off significantly in the amount of material you can retain from the lecture. Then at least once a week, you can briefly review the lecture using this same approach, with special attention to those questions that you have difficulty answering.

Tips on note taking. Here are some general principles for good note-taking. We recommend taking notes in a bound spiral notebook rather than using loose leaf paper. One of the things that can happen when you use loose leaf paper is that notes can be misplaced or lost. Using a bound spiral notebook insures that the notes will always be in sequence, and you won't lose individual pages. Notes should be taken with a pen, not with a pencil to insure they will remain clearly legible. Also, make sure that your handwriting is readable, otherwise your notes provide no benefit. So take the time to make your handwriting clear. Start each daily note with a title, date and the name of the lecturer. Number your pages across the top corner, so the sequence is maintained. As indicated above, write your notes using three to five word key word phrases, and keep the notes simple to understand. Use key words that the instructor uses and that make sense to you. Make sure to use an organizational structure with indentation, where appropriate. Be sure to leave plenty of space for clarifying or expanding what you have written during class at some later date while you are studying. Finally, diagrams and drawings should be positioned near the appropriate content area, so that it is easy to link information in your notes with the diagrams or drawings. Good note taking skills are a foundation for efficient learning. A good hint is to use nouns, verbs and adjectives/adverbs – minimize your use of prepositions (of, with) and conjunctions (e.g., the).

Avoid wasting time recopying notes. Spending extra time recopying notes is not an efficient nor is it a fun strategy for learning. Instead, highlight important points in your notes and use this information as a focus for your studying. Although recopying notes is not recommended, it can be helpful to review notes with the intention of adding highlighted material from the readings. That means when you are reading assignments your class notes should be readily available so you can transfer information as needed. You should realize that your notes are your STUDY GUIDE, and the text is a resource from which you add important information to your STUDY GUIDE. In that way you're integrating information you have read with information that you have heard. Remember, it is not a good use of your time to just re-copy notes. There are much better strategies for remembering information. Use your text and notes to build a STUDY GUIDE which serves as a condensed version of the material. Then use your STUDY GUIDE to study more efficiently.

"Build your STUDY GUIDE from your notes and readings."

13. Learn from a Visit with a Professor. At this point in our discussion it is helpful to talk about the value of visiting personally with your teacher or professor. Most students do not take advantage of this key resource for

learning. Taking the time to meet your teacher or professor, one-on-one, will first of all give them an opportunity to know who you are, and you can begin to establish a personal relationship so that s/he will recognize you in class. Second, it will provide you with insight into what the teacher or professor considers to be important in life and in class as you listen and observe the surroundings. Often times in the course of conversation with your teacher or professor, you will find that the professor will communicate important ideas about the course content that will find their way into the tests. In addition, the teacher or professor can be a source of guidance and counsel about what and how to study. Getting to know your professor will also provide an opportunity for you to receive general guidance and advice for success in college. Regular visits with the teacher or professor will affirm that you are an interested and engaged learner who wants to get all that you can out of your education.

"Visit with your professor early and regularly during a course."

Summary Habit 2:

- Use SQ3R method of study for learning from written material and a set of strategies for learning from lectures.

- Be efficient with your time.

- Review what you've learned as soon as possible after you have learned it.

- Gain more by visiting with your professor.

HABIT 3

Organize yourself.

Get it right from the textbook and in-class

In this chapter you will learn the importance of:

1) Setting goals
2) Understanding classroom expectations
3) Implementing time management
4) Creating a good learning environment
5) Planning ahead for your best performance.

I love being organized!

Joe, a 20 year old student, just failed a microbiology test and came to me for advice. His score on the examination before the curve was a 54%, after the curve it was raised to 60%. During the interview, Joe admitted that he didn't read the five assigned chapters; he just skimmed them and focused on what he thought was important in each chapter. He read the objectives and tried to address the objectives by skimming the chapter. He just listened during each lecture; he didn't take class notes. Instead, he borrowed lecture notes from a classmate. He watched the baseball World Series several nights before the examination, including the night before the exam. He studied by himself by quietly reading the material. Where did Joe go wrong?

There are many places Joe went wrong. Overall, his plan of attack was way off. He was poorly prepared, he learned only a portion of the information, his study methods were inefficient and he prioritized baseball viewing as being more important than exam performance. Further, his coming for help after a poor performance (instead of preparing beforehand and introducing himself early in the course), was indicative of **poor organization as well as *reactive* behavior.** You will do much better in school by exhibiting ***proactive*** behavior instead of reactive behavior. Here are techniques for putting proactive behavior into practice.

Are you proactive or reactive?

1. **Be proactive.** Actions have consequences. The consequences you experience are the results of you being either proactive or reactive. Being proactive is making choices, accepting *responsibility*, and not blaming others. Being proactive allows you to recognize things you can control, plan events in advance, and plan their potential outcome. Being proactive is the first habit defined in the book, *The 7 Habits of Highly Effective Teens*, authored by Sean Covey. It is an important step in taking responsibility for one's actions and in one's life. We agree with Sean that 'being proactive' is an extremely important step in improving almost all outcomes with situations you will encounter. If you want favorable outcomes, be proactive. Plan in advance and set goals.

Table 1. Proactive behaviors to employ and reactive behaviors to avoid.

PROACTIVE	REACTIVE
Organizing class materials in advance	Looking for class materials amongst a pile
Separating class materials into folders	Mixing notes from several classes
Reading a chapter before class	Looking for a pen/book during class
Memorizing a key concept the night before	Trying to write a response during a pop quiz when you haven't studied

We are not alone in this view. Sir Winston Churchill said, "The price of greatness is responsibility." And, in terms of academics, if you want to perform at a great level (i.e., excellence) then it is your responsibility to do so. In contrast, if you do not accept responsibility for your academic performance, then you are forever playing defense and reacting to poor grades. That is where Joe found himself, in a position of defense, in a professor's office after failing a microbiology examination as a result of not being proactive.

"It is your responsibility to perform at a high level."

Proactive Behavior #1: Set Your Goals. Taking control of your academic performance begins with setting goals. By setting goals you are being proactive and taking steps in **predicting your classroom performance.** Underlying this is your foundation – your level of motivation to do well in a course – how much value you place on your performance. In Chapter 1, we discussed motivation and its importance in determining academic success. We asked you to answer the question, "What are your academic ambitions?"

Hopefully, by now you are becoming convinced of the value of good academic outcomes and you are answering this question with "I want A's in all my courses because that reflects I have learned the material well." Remember, you will likely achieve only the goals that you set. Once you set your goals, be proactive by **scheduling time to study regularly,** thinking about the class and getting assignments done. As you will see below, regular study time does not mean a lot of dedicated time. In fact, many of the best students can study in a minimum amount of time. And, we want to show you how to be efficient with your study time.

Proactive Behavior #2: Understand Classroom Expectations. At the outset of a new class you will often be provided a course outline or syllabus that details the required book, topics to be covered, the sequence, when tests or quizzes are to be given, how much each test/quiz is worth, and the evaluation method. Rules about attendance, assignments and classroom behavior also appear in the course syllabus. Be aware that the course syllabus is a contract between you and the instructor. And, by the nature of a contract, it is a binding agreement between two or more parties. Thus, it serves as the basis of your final evaluation by your teacher. To be successful, you need to understand what is expected of you as stated in the syllabus. So, **read** the course syllabus. **Pay close attention** to the syllabus. **Keep** the course syllabus (do not throw it away). **Keep** all documents for that class in one location[1] and **refer** to the course syllabus as often as you need. You should check your understanding of the syllabus by identifying when important test dates occur (mark them on your calendar; yes, you need to have a personal calendar!), what you will be responsible for (assignments, quizzes and tests), and how the final grade is calculated. If you are not sure about any aspect of the syllabus or course requirements, you should ask the teacher to clarify or ask a fellow student who you can trust to provide accurate advice.

Don't be like one of our sons, who said in the 7th grade, "I threw out the course syllabus" (classic behavior that many failing college undergraduates also demonstrate!). He didn't think it was important. However, he soon found out that he didn't know when assignments were due, when quizzes occurred, and when tests were coming. The syllabus helps you plan ahead for these important events.

The proactive student keeps all the materials from one class in one location/folder. This means that you have to have a binder or expandable folder for every class. Mixing paperwork up amongst your classes is the route to disaster. You need to be able to locate the course syllabus, assignments, lecture notes and old exams quickly and efficiently if you want to succeed.

"The course syllabus is a contract between you and the instructor. Use the syllabus to plan ahead."

Classroom expectations are often defined further during lectures by the instructor throughout the semester. To ensure good performance, pay particular attention to the instructor who details assignments, that is due dates, page length, line spacing and font (i.e., typing) requirements for that assignment. Also, virtually all instructors mention the chapters to be covered on upcoming quizzes/exams, the time allotment for the quizzes/exams and the examination format (fill in the blank, short answer, essay, computer format, bubble sheet/electronic grading) either in the syllabus or during a classroom session. Pay close attention to these comments and write them down. Be responsible for knowing this information well in advance of the due date of the assignment.

"Academically successful students know what is due, when it is due, and how his/her performance will be measured."

Proactive Behavior #3: Get the Required Books. One aspect of being organized is having the materials needed for each course. Start with the basics. Have pencils, pens, highlighters, paper and folder and notebooks. Then get the right book for the course. Instructors in college will list the books required for their course in their syllabus. They will also list books that are recommended. As part of your educational experience, you will be asked to make more and more decisions that will have consequences regarding your academic career. One of these decisions is whether to buy the required book(s) and recommended books.

Generally speaking, professors **use the required books for a reason** – that is it is *their favorite source for test materials*. In contrast, **recommended book(s)** are used as complementary readings that provide additional context, information or points of view.

"Understand the value of buying and reading the required textbook."

There is no substitute for having the required book for the course. First of all, the instructor's statement that "this book is required" means that s/he feels that the required "book" is important for your full understanding of a given topic. Don't underestimate their many years of experience of selecting the best text for the course. In fact, the required book may have been written by the professor or one of his/her colleagues. Nevertheless, every year students try to "get by" without buying the required textbook. Let us relate a couple of true short stories about students who did not understand the value of buying and reading the required textbook.

Cases of Not Getting the Required Book

Case 1. Jonathan, a 18 year old freshman college student, "Dr. C. do I really need the book? Don't the handouts that you provide contain all the important information?"

Case 2. Sheila, 19 year old college student, approached her professor sheepishly after the second exam stating, "Dr. C. I don't think I have the right book for your course."

Case 3. Matthew, a 23 year old dental student, asked me, "Dr. C. I see in the course syllabus that you recommend the 6th edition of your textbook, however I have the 5th edition. Is the 5th edition okay?"

In Case 1, Jonathan assumes that all the important material appears in the handouts, when in fact, handouts often only summarize key points. The details and important facts appear in the book. **Solution: "Buy the required book!"**

In Sheila's case, making a discovery that you have the wrong book after the second examination is a big mistake. Semester long courses often have 3 to 5 exams, so realizing this mistake after exam 2, means that she has already jeopardized about 40% of her final grade. **Solution: "Buy the right book!"**

Case 3 illustrates the thought that no new information appears in the 6th edition since the 5th edition was published 5 years before. This is illogical.

For example, "does 5 years make a difference for other things in your life, such as popular songs and artists, buying music or the hand-held devices that store these items? Is the price, method for purchasing these items and method of electronic storage the same today as it was 5 or 10 years ago?" We believe you understand our point, with the bottom line being 'things change', 'information changes' and 'books change'. Keep in mind also that there are a variety of ways to save money when buying the right books. Buying on-line or the right 'used' book can save serious money!

"Buy the most current edition as recommended by the instructor as cost effectively as you can."

Proactive Behavior #4: Manage Your Time. Almost all books on the topic of being successful mention time management. It is clearly recognized by experts to be an essential tool for success in life and academic performance. In today's world, time management is important because of the rapid pace of our society and constant selection of things to do. These selections must be balanced with the demands of getting an education.

2. Take control of your schedule. Taking control of your schedule requires you to balance your time between studying and social activities, family, a job, and likely many other things. Because of these choices and potential pressures associated with not giving up anything, you must learn to take control of your schedule to get the most out of your educational experience. Trust us, taking control of your time in an organized manner will reduce the amount of time you need to study so you work more efficiently, your performance improves and you have time for those important extracurricular activities. As a result of learning how to manage your time effectively, you will reduce your daily stress and achieve the academic successes you hope for with minimum amount of effort.

Time management does not require a complex formula. It only requires 4 things and about 2 minutes a day. The four things are:

1. Knowing what needs to be done
2. A calendar
3. A list of things to do – recorded and prioritized
4. Regular/Daily use of this habit

Use a 2 by 4 to build your academic structure. Think of time management as a 2 by 4, which in carpenter terms is a piece of lumber that is used as a basic structure for building. If you want to build academic success use your 2 by 4 to structure your time daily and build a structure of success.

Okay, let's demonstrate how it works. First, you begin by writing down what needs to be done. There are 2 categories for this task. 1) Things that need to be done in days or weeks to come, and 2) tasks that need to be done today. Let's start with the items due in days or weeks. These deadlines might be assignments, such as term papers, posters, presentations, quizzes or exams. To tackle these, get a calendar that goes for at least the semester, so you can plan ahead. This will serve as your **master schedule.** The calendar can be big or small and can be portable or hang on your wall. Size is not important, only that you use it and you can readily get to it. One advantage of carrying a portable calendar is that it keeps you organized, it is easy to manage and it travels with you wherever you go.

Plan your master schedule.
As soon as your courses begin, ideally during the first week of each semester, get out each course syllabus and record all of the dates of quizzes and tests on to your **monthly calendar.** Next, record the due dates of all other assignments. Record all quizzes and tests in one color and all other assignments due in another. This gives you an overall feel for which weeks will be important. Place the calendar (i.e., your master schedule) in a location where you can **see it each day.**

Get in the habit of checking your calendar at the beginning of each week and every school day morning. You need to look at the calendar to see the things that are coming due. Plan your week accordingly, that way no assignment sneaks up on you, and YOU have control of your schedule.

3. Write down daily tasks. For the daily tasks, we suggest that you use a portable calendar or an electronic task manager located on your phone or hand-held device. Another simple method uses post-it size pieces of paper that you place in a location readily available to you each morning. The size of the paper should allow you to write at least 5 tasks per day. Place a small stack of these papers where you can conveniently write your "to dos" each morning, and replenish the stack as needed. Some convenient locations to place these blank sheets include your desk, your bedroom dresser or bathroom counter. I personally like to plan my list every morning in the shower. When I get out of the shower, I usually write down the 2 to 5 things I need and want to accomplish that day. I call this list my **To Do Today (TDT)** list. It takes me about 1 minute to jot these items down. Then, double check your master calendar for any additional major items coming this week, and add those items to the list. Then prioritize which items are most important to get done first by numbering the items in the sequence of priority. That takes about one more minute. Then, place the list in your pocket, purse, phone or backpack and take it with you. Portability of the list is important, that is why it is suggested that the list be kept on small pieces of paper or in a portable organizer. When you arrive at your class or study destination, check your list and begin accomplishing your tasks. When you complete a task, check it off the list. One of the reasons I like to use a portable organizer is that you can look back and see what you have successfully accomplished in a day, week, or month! This *glance at the past* also gives you a sense of accomplishment and is positive feedback that the method is working.

"Make a TDT list and limit it to no more than 5 school-related tasks daily."

Note to be successful at this technique you should limit the number of 'school-related' tasks to about 5 each day. By having too many tasks, you are unlikely to accomplish all of them that can lead to a bit of frustration. So be reasonable when making your TDT each morning. In the case where you have items left on your list, place your list next to your blank TDT sheets at the end of each day, then transfer those unaccomplished items to your TDT the next morning. You should realize that your list can have non-study items on it, like "do laundry", "play b-ball", "meet Joe at 6 pm." These non-study items are fine, however they can complicate days already packed with lots to do. Try to avoid giving yourself too many tasks or errands especially if a test, quiz or major assignment is due. For example, on days just before a test, you should limit your TDT to 2 items so you allow plenty of time for studying. Also, to make this habit work best, check your master schedule each morning before completing your TDT so you transfer important tasks from your master schedule to your TDT.

"Transfer important tasks from your master schedule to your TDT."

Key points to this technique include creating your calendar once every day (TDT), prioritizing the list, carrying your list (and a calendar) with you daily, and checking off the items as you go. You should record items as soon as you learn or think of them (note that can be as soon as you get out of the shower), and remember that teachers may make new assignments during class, so you need to add these to your master calendar when you arrive back at your room/home. For these cases, by carrying the TDT with you, you can add new entries as you go.

"Carry your TDT so you can add new entries and add important tasks to your master schedule." [2]

4. Create a learning environment. To study effectively and do well in school, you need a learning environment that fits your learning style. Selecting the site where you study is important. A noisy place where a lot of people are milling about or gathering can be distracting if you need a quiet setting. On the other

---

Visit our web-site called the "MinedStore" www.minedstore.com where you can purchase sticky notes for our TDTs. Alternatively, there are plenty of other websites like Daytimers.com where you can purchase organizational materials and calendars.

hand, you may study best in a setting with background noise like music, a fan, or even white noise. Therefore, you should select a place that works for you - realizing a quiet indoor site often gives you greater control of several things including the temperature, lighting and amount of distractions and noise present. However, a nice quiet place under a tree can be fine, but it can also be an inviting place for friends to see you and stop by for a chat. Whether your study site is quiet or one with some background noise, you should find the right place for doing your best work and then use that place for your regular study.

Along with the right amount of quiet that suits you, you need a study site that has good lighting and is comfortable. Select a study site that has enough lighting to see easily the text in your books, but avoid light that produces a glare off the pages. Your study site should allow you to place both your book and notes out in front you. While reading the text, you can then refer to your notes for clarification or to add information you just read from the text to your notes. You should sit upright against a firm back in the chair and have a comfortable seat. Lounging on a sofa or bed is not conducive for reading course material or studying. Please note that many "C" students tout this lounging technique as one of their favorites.

"Study in the right environment."

5. Don't be distracted. Learning and studying requires concentration. Thus, being free from distractions is a goal. Distractions can be external or internal. External distractions come in the form of people and in today's world electronics and motorized objects. You should limit exposure to these factors during studying even though you may believe that you can study with background auditory or visual noise. So, turn off the TV, radio, iPod and your telephone. This limits exposure to other people and sounds during your studying. You can turn your portable electronics back on as soon as you are done studying. And, since **we recommend studying in short bursts** you can check your phone, or interact with others after 30 minutes of study.

Internal distractions often come in the form of anxiety, stress or a mind that is wandering to other things besides studying. Your anxiety and stress levels can often be regulated by simple breathing exercises (see paragraph below entitled, Your Brain and proper breathing). Remember that your brain is like a TV, only there is no "off" button. You have to use the channel selector to put your mind on what you want to be thinking about. There is no value in letting distractions or repetitive negative thoughts have control of your internal TV screen (i.e., your brain).

"Be distraction free during studying."

Special distractions. A special distraction worth mentioning here is email, texting and various social networks and electronic games on your phone, computer, or TV. These activities, although enjoyable can be very time consuming. Often people will spend hours doing these activities at the expense of studying. If you must email, text or play an electronic game, you should schedule the activity for a specific time and limit the activity to no more than one hour each day. Email is best checked once or twice each weekday; some prefer checking around 9:30 a.m. and once after 4 p.m. At these times, others have generally sent you their communications of importance. Checking more often is too time consuming. Limit your emailing to 20 minute sessions. Electronic gaming is often played during times when it is perceived that nothing else needs to be done. However, this type of distraction should be engaged only after checking your TDT and master schedule for items of importance and items left on the list. If items remain, those should be accomplished first. Limiting the amount of time with these distractions will lead to better academic performance.

6. **Study regularly.** To plan for optimum performance you need to study regularly. Regularly means on a consistent basis. Regularly means you think about school every weekday. As you think about school, those thoughts should be about 'what are my assignments and tasks?' and 'when are they due?' These tasks should then appear on your TDT. In turn, your TDT influences the regularity of your studying.

Regularly means having a specific location for studying. You should have one preferred site where you like to study. This is where you go when you want to concentrate and focus on studying. When you arrive, your mind should equate the location with the word "study." This is where you get your work done.

You should regularly dedicate time to study at your study location. Now don't be turned off here. We are not recommending dedicating a lot of time to studying. Instead, we recommend a little bit every day. And, there is also a bit of flexibility here. Here is how this works.

"A regular study plan and environment is conducive for good grades."

Plan the time of day and amount of time for studying each day. For example, you have written on your TDT "*study history*" which means you need to accomplish this task today, but you have all day to do it. There may be some time in the afternoon or evening to accomplish this task. Once you identify the time best for you, write the time next to the task "*study history 3 pm or b4 dinner.*" Then go to "*your study site*" a few minutes before that time and get organized.

Set your study materials out and begin the task. Remember 30 minute bursts are recommended followed by short breaks. If you have a lot on your TDT, then dedicate up to 2, 30 minute sessions per topic, then move to a new topic after a 5  minute break. If you only have a few items on your TDT, then you can spend up to 90 minutes (i.e., three 30 minute study bursts with breaks in between) on the topic. After that, move on to other extracurricular things and enjoy the other things life has to offer.

7. Create a routine to maximize self-regulatory control. There are additional things that you can do to maximize your control over learning new material. These include getting exercise, getting good nutrition, getting quality sleep, and knowing how to regulate your mind and body.

Physical activity. During adolescence and the first few years of college, many students gain weight. In fact, there is a term known as the "freshman ten" because many freshmen put on 10 pounds of additional weight as they adjust to the new demands and social infrastructure of college. Extra weight can be in the form of fat or muscle depending on how you metabolize the food and whether or not you exercise. Exercising is beneficial because it increases the production of endorphins and minimizes weight gain, both of which make you feel better. Exercise also enhances your self-image, your desire and your ability to accomplish things - which is the attitude needed to do well in school. There is plenty of evidence to suggest that keeping in good physical condition leads to optimum performance mentally and physically. Most experts recommend that you exercise for at least 30 minutes at least 3 times weekly, but this is now considered the bare minimum as recent evidence suggests that we should perform vigorous physical activity at least 5 days per week. This can be in the form of jogging or walking, cycling, swimming laps, lifting weights, dancing, or playing a recreational sport (preferably on most days of the week). You should target moderate intensity during the session to gain mental and physical benefit. Be aware, moderate intensity is often defined as a target walking speed of 3.5 miles per hour, bicycling at 12 miles per hour, swimming laps with moderate effort, or more simply - activity that makes you out of breath or sweaty. These activities will cause you to burn between 100 and 250 calories per 30 minute session (based on an average weight of between 120 and 175 pounds).

On some days, you may find that you don't have enough time to exercise. However, all is not lost. Be flexible and creative. For example, on a day in which your TDT is full, and time does not permit you to complete a 30 minute exercise session, then you can split exercise over multiple sessions during the day, or use your 5 minute breaks between studying to do push-ups, sit-ups, step-ups, dancing, or walking up and down stairs. The latter is one of the many overlooked ways to exercise, that is the stairs. Many buildings at schools have stairs, but often people take elevators. Take the stairs every chance you have to get your exercise. If you have a lot of flights to climb, take it slow at first. Over many days of stair climbing you will build strength and confidence. Other ways of getting exercise include riding a bike to class, carrying a backpack with

a few books in it (don't over do it of course…we have a life rule about taking care of yourself), and taking a longer (but safe) path when walking home from class.

Nutrition and the intelligent diet. There is no lack of books on the topic of nutrition and weight loss, and many experts on the topic. However, few students realize the importance of a good diet to help your mind think. Okay, let us explain. Brain function (i.e., thinking) requires communication between neural pathways and also energy for the brain cells to function. Let's talk about the communication first. Communication between neurons requires biochemical messengers that transmit signals. These messengers, called neurotransmitters, come in three forms: acetylcholine, dopamine and serotonin. Substances that help make up these neurotransmitters are found in the foods you should eat. For example if you eat eggs, milk, cheese, peanuts, wheat germ, meat, fish, and vegetables you are building up supplies of acetylcholine. Proteins (meat, milk products, fish, beans, nuts, soy products) provide you the materials to make dopamine. And, carbohydrates like breads, cereals, pasta, potatoes, starchy vegetables, and chocolate help construct serotonin.

"Eat well so your brain has the energy to perform at its optimum."

Once you have the necessary neurotransmitters, energy is needed for the brain cells to send the signals from neuron to neuron. Energy comes from the food you eat, the glucose you absorb and the oxygen you breathe. Accordingly, you should eat moderate portions, at regular times (limit snacks), and include protein, cereals, whole grains, and don't forget to eat fruit and vegetables daily.

Most experts recommend 3-4 ounces of protein at meals (don't over do it) per day. Also, the daily consumption of four ounces of cereals and whole grains, and three to four servings of fruits and vegetables is recommended. These foods are high in vitamin B complex, vitamin C, minerals and antioxidants that are important for your brain to function at its best. Of course, the amount you eat depends on the amount of calories you burn and excrete daily – so bigger, more active individuals will obviously need more food than smaller less active persons. Gauge yourself accordingly. Interestingly, recent research has found that your ability to self regulate (as an example, sit yourself down to study and actually do so!) is linked to the level of brain fuel (glucose) available. When blood glucose levels are low, it is more difficult to have "will power" or self regulate. So, make sure that you regularly eat a well-balanced diet so that your brain has adequate energy to perform at its optimum. Also, after big meals much of your oxygenated blood is being diverted to your stomach to help digest the food. We recommend that you eat small meals before studying, to avoid that sleepy feeling after a big meal.

"Eat small but nutritious meals before studying – avoid big meals before studying."

You should drink water to be fully hydrated and to provide sufficient blood for circulation to, in and around your brain. At least 1 liter every 8 hours is recommended. We're not big fans of carbonated beverages, either diet or non-diet, for a growing list of reasons that include taking in large amounts of caffeine regularly and high concentration of

calories in non-diet sodas. But, you may find the use of sports drinks containing glucose to be a helpful supplement to your functioning when you study for long periods or have to take an extended exam.

Your brain and proper breathing. Oxygen is important for proper brain function, but so is keeping the right amount of carbon dioxide in your blood. By breathing correctly you can control the level of these gases in your bloodstream. For example, breathing with your diaphragm is helpful for calming the body and allowing oxygen to be available for the brain. Quite often because of the stress of life, the way we breathe shifts from using mostly the diaphragm to movements using the upper chest. If you find that your breathing is mostly with your chest, you may want to learn how to breathe more regularly with your diaphragm – in which your stomach gently rises with each breath inward and gently falls as air is released outward - by taking a yoga class or by visiting with a health provider who can help you relearn proper breathing techniques. This kind of diaphragmatic breathing when done slowly and with a relaxed feeling will help you better control your stress level and give you an increased ability to quiet yourself.

It is important note that diaphragmatic/relaxation breathing may require you seeking the help of a qualified health professional to learn how to breathe in a relaxed manner.

"Slow, relaxed breathing can affect how your brain functions."

Quality sleep. Getting a good night's sleep is also important for good academic performance and should not be underestimated. Sufficient sleep means going to bed at a regular time and getting enough sleep to feel rested. For most of us, this means somewhere between 7 and 9 hours every night. This amount of time provides adequate rest for your mind and body. To get this amount of sleep, it means you need to avoid staying up late on a frequent basis and pulling "all nighters" to study and cram. Fortunately, the study methods in this book when used correctly should prevent your need to cram and stay up late at night, unless it is for a special occasion.

There are several things that you can do that will favor falling to sleep and getting a good night's rest. One thing you can do to produce quality sleep is to get regular exercise. Regular physical activity and exercise increases your core temperature and sends oxygenated blood to your body tissues and brain. After exercise, your body is fatigued and wants rest. Exercise can promote sleep when performed regularly and at the right time of day. Exercise should be performed well before bedtime - at least 3 hrs before bedtime – to give you enough time to gear down and cool down from that activity.

"Get good quality sleep to favor getting your best academic performance."

Another controllable factor regarding quality of sleep is what you do during the hour before going to bed. In addition to limiting exercise at this time, watching an athletic event or horror movie right before bed can make it difficult to fall asleep. Both events can produce a lot of anxiety and emotional swings that are not beneficial for sleep and should be avoided especially the night before a quiz or examination.

Summary Habit 3:

- Get organized. This is defined by your ability to be proactive, plan in advance and give your body and mind the opportunity to perform at its best.

- By using your "to do today (TDT)" list, eating a nutritious diet, taking the time to exercise, getting the proper amount of sleep, and controlling your stress level you will find time to study regularly using a mind and body that is readily receptive to learning new information.

- Once you are organized, you are now ready to learn habit 4 – how to prepare for exams.

HABIT 4

Prepare for exams.

In this chapter you will learn the importance of:

1) Planning and preparation
2) Identifying the important material
3) Condensing the information
4) Using good memorization skills
5) Predicting test questions in advance.

Brother 1 and brother 2 were roommates in college. Brother 1, the older, had his college classes well under control with an A average and was eyeing graduation within a month. Brother 2, the younger, was also doing quite well but was under the pressure of an exam the next day and was being pestered by his older brother to get out on the town that evening with friends. It was 7 pm and brother 2 had yet to study for the evening but had been preparing all week for the exam. Brother 1 came back from a shower after a workout and dinner and started bugging brother 2 to get moving because the party started soon. Within 10 minutes, other friends arrived at the doorway asking brother 2 if he was coming. Brother 2 quickly pulled out his study sheet, reviewed the information on it and within 5 minutes stated, "I am ready for my exam, let's go!" The next day brother 2 confidently took the exam, and received a 98%. His friends, who saw him study for only 5 minutes were amazed by his performance. How did he do so well? The secrets lie ahead in this chapter.

Success begins on day 1: planning, preparing and training.

The above story illustrates the importance of **early planning and preparation**. By the time 'crunch time' arrived, that is the day before the exam, brother 2 had already prepared sufficiently for the exam. Yes, studying requires good preparation much like preparing for an athletic event or competition. To be successful you need to prepare in advance, have a schedule, take measure of the volume of material being tested, and know what to do at each training session. So, **studying is planning, preparing, measuring and training.**

"Measure the volume."

The amount of material that appears on an exam varies from class to class. Because of this, you must measure the volume of material that will appear on each exam. By this, we mean, measure the number of lecture hours being covered on each exam. Often teachers will test students every 5 to 10 lecture hours, which may be anywhere from 1 to 10 chapters. However, other classes test every 20 to 40 hours of lecture and **you have to make adjustments** based on this simple fact. Once you have tabulated the number of lecture hours that will be on the exam, we suggest multiplying this by 2 to give you the number of hours you should study for the exam. So, a test that covers 8 hours of lecture generally requires about 16 hours of studying. To squeeze these 16 hours in, you may have to spend 2 hours a day reading and reviewing your notes, building a study guide, and quizzing yourself as described in this chapter. Only you know how best to divide those hours. However, we have found that most students spread half of the studying out several days before the exam, and the **last two days before the exam are reserved for final preparation.** Thus, if you follow these guidelines then 2 to 3 hours of time set aside the last few days before the exam should be sufficient, and part of your plan.

"Train your brain."

After measuring the volume of material (# of lecture hours), you need to train your brain to think about information that will be on the exam, if you want to do well on the exam. Training is a regular event that requires discipline and dedication. We suspect you can't imagine running 10 miles without first training and getting your body and legs into shape. Think similarly about your exams. Your reading sessions are like jogging short distances. Attending class and taking notes is another training session. And, reviewing your notes is a further training session. Eventually these training sessions – over several weeks - increase your knowledge, just as you would increase your running distance each week to get to your 10 mile goal.

"Studying requires training your brain at regular intervals – just like training for a long distance run."

1. Plan and prepare. Let's start with preparation. First and foremost is knowing the date of the exam. At the beginning of each course and as soon as you learn of the date of your exams, you should create a **MASTER SCHEDULE** by marking your monthly calendar with all the exam dates. A calendar is key, since you will plan specific things to do and study each week to be properly prepare.

Pay particular attention to how many exams fall each week. One exam per week is often very manageable. However, be

Master Calendar Schedule							
	MON	TUES	WED	THUR	FRI	SAT	SUN
7-10 AM		Class		Class			
10-Noon			Class				
Lunch							
1-3 PM	Study Math	Study Math	Study Math		Free Time		
3-6 PM	Free Time	Class	Visit Professor	Class		Free Time	
Dinner							
7-10 PM	Study Chemistry		Study Chemistry		Study Chemistry		

aware that in college often several exams occur in the same week, and that is especially true for midterms and finals. So, when this occurs you really need to plan and prepare in advance.

Planning and preparation for exams require several key events that are easy to accomplish. They include the following sequential events:

1. **Get and use a monthly calendar**
2. **Know when the exam is and mark your calendar**
3. **Obtain the book**
4. **Read the assignment / chapter(s) in advance**
5. **Obtain notes from lectures.**
6. **Identify what's important.**
7. **Manage the information: condense and reduce what you need to know by building a STUDY GUIDE.**
8. **Memorize the important material in the STUDY GUIDE.**
9. **Periodically review the important information.**
10. **Identify what you don't know.**
11. **Study what you don't know.**
12. **Cross the finish line.**

In the previous chapters, we already discussed the importance of having the book, reading the chapters and taking good notes. We also emphasized the importance of creating a good learning environment, studying regularly in short bursts, and using your TDT list to stay on track. Now let's go back to the point about highlighting. **Remember you are highlighting information that you find important and you need to know for the exam.** You can highlight, underline or mark in the margin the important points, whatever method you like best. But make it your **goal to find at least one important fact or concept per page.** Often there is one main thought per paragraph and at least 3 to 4 important facts per page. Try not to highlight everything on the page because this indicates that you are not separating what is important from what is not.

"Find and highlight the important facts in each paragraph."

As you read the chapter, you should have your notes close by. Refer to your notes to add understanding to the chapter reading. Also, highlight the important concepts in your notes. As you finish each page, take a moment to think over the important (highlighted) points. Think how each highlighted point relates to what the chapter is about and what you have previously read. Think how this fact (or concept) inter-relates with other important facts on the page, on previous pages, and in your notes. It may be helpful to draw a diagram or illustration that shows the linkage between the important points so you have a clear understanding of the subject. Put the main idea at the top or center of the diagram and relate the subordinate facts so you generate a full concept of the subject. Although this method may seem to slow you down, by identifying the main thoughts and taking time to recall this information, you are actually adding efficiency by learning while you study.

> ## "After finishing each page, take a moment to think about the important (highlighted) points and inter-relate them by drawing a diagram or figure."

2. Identify what is important. Teachers write test questions to evaluate your knowledge of the topic. The majority of questions focus on important information they want you to know and retain for a long time. As a student, it is helpful for you to think about the information in such a way that you can identify the important information.

In the classroom. To test well, you need to know "what is important", that is the main thoughts. Important information can be identified in several ways including during lecture, from the notes or textbook, and from interacting with the teacher or classmates. One of the easiest methods for identifying important information is to pay attention during daily classroom lectures. Teacher often provide obvious clues to what is important by saying things like, "write (jot) this down", "this is important" "you need to know this. . .", "this would make a good test question", or they may be a bit more subtle and mention a fact or

concept more than once (i.e., repeating). Sometimes teachers will relate the fact to another concept indicating its importance. Ideally, when these verbal cues are given by the teacher, you should write the fact down and put an asterisk (*) by it that indicates that the teacher emphasized this fact as being important. When you return to your notes, you will see these asterisks (*) and that will make the job of identifying the important stuff that much easier.

"Listen to the teacher: important facts or concepts are often repeated and related to another important concept."

Another way to identify important material is to identify the major points provided during the summary of each lecture. Instructors often post summary slides during the final 5 minutes of class that emphasize the main points of that day's lecture. Make sure you get this information recorded and place asterisks next to this information to indicate its importance. Then, before leaving the classroom, spend a few minutes thinking about how the summary points tie to the information provided during the beginning and middle portions of that day's lecture.

"Important information is often mentioned during the summary at the end of a lecture."

Assigned readings. As part of the learning process, it is important to ensure on a weekly basis that you are on track. Plan to do the assigned reading so there is sufficient time to review what you have learned. For example, if the test is covering 4 chapters and you have 4 weeks to prepare, use a calendar to plan for this important event. You should plan on having all your reading done at least one week prior to the exam. Then during the last week you can focus on the important information you identified during your weekly reading.

Monday	Tuesday	Wednesday	Thursday	Friday	Saturday	Sunday
1	2	3	4	5 FINISH STUDY GUIDE	6	7
8	9 REVIEW STUDY GUIDE	10	11 STUDY CONCEPTS I DON'T KNOW YET	12	13 EXAM	14
15	16	17	18	19	20	21

Finding important information in assigned readings is guided by similar principles as those applied during the lectures, except the main concepts appear within the text. When reading the chapter, it is your job to find the main thoughts in the readings. Here are three ways to identify important points in assigned readings.

1. The first way is to limit the incoming information to small domains (chunks) or passages. This is easier to conceptualize if you realize that textbooks have standard divisions. For example, textbooks are typically divided into chapters, chapters are usually divided into sections, and sections contain one or more paragraphs. Each chapter and section is generally loaded with lots of facts that can be a bit overwhelming to learn. So, make it easy on yourself and target the small stuff first. Don't worry about the entire chapter or even all the sections. Take the first section that you read and break it down into paragraphs. Realize that there is likely at least one important point per paragraph. Now read the paragraph and find the important point.

> ### "In books and readings, there is likely at least one important point per paragraph…find it."

Here is an example from a standard book:

DRUG INTERACTIONS (from Yagiela JA, Neidle EN, Dowd FJ: *Pharmacology and Therapeutics for Dentistry*, 4th edition, Mosby, 1998, p. 346)

"Antiarrhythmic drugs can participate in a wide variety of drug interactions. Because the margin of safety with these drugs (antiarrhythmic) as a group is narrow, clinically significant interactions may develop whenever the activity or plasma concentration of an antiarrhythmic agent is disturbed. The following discussion is intended to provide an illustrative but not exhaustive list of interactions involving these drugs."

In this case, we have highlighted the important points of the paragraph. If you were to summarize the paragraph you would write 12 words that summarize a 60 word paragraph. Notice how we substantially **condensed the information** in the summary outline on the next page.

Drug Interactions

Antiarrhythmic drugs

1. *narrow margin of safety*
2. *plasma concentration disturbed*

by : 1. 2. 3.

(1, 2, 3 are drug names based on the information in the next few paragraphs).

"Reduce the amount to read by 4/5 (80%) by condensing and summarizing."

As you can see, standard paragraphs provide text that lead up to the important point. The main point may be new information or information you already know. You want to focus on the new information. Because "lead up" information is less important than the main thought, this may require you to vary the rate of your reading such that things familiar can be read rapidly and the main points (or more difficult points) read more carefully (i.e., slowly) with underlining or highlighting.

"Vary your rate of reading so main points are read more carefully and highlighted."

Once you have identified the new information, highlight the keywords in the sentence. Note in the example above, we only highlighted the words "activity", "plasma concentration" and disturbed" as being the keywords. Focusing on keywords helps in your study efficiency. And, if you don't know the meaning of a particular word, then you should look up the definition of these keywords and terms, or ask a friend or the instructor to make sure you have full understanding of the main thought.

> "Focus on the new information, by identifying keywords, highlighting keywords, and knowing the definitions of the keywords."

Section headers. Section headers provide context for the information that follows, and provide useful clues as to what is coming and what should be learned. It is important for you to understand that the important information is directly linked to the section header. For example, the section header in our paragraph described above is "DRUG INTERACTIONS." These two words mean you should be looking for important drug interactions, what drugs cause them, what is the cause of drug interactions, and what is the result of the interactions? Asking questions like these makes you an active **reader** and is very helpful for identifying the important information.

> "Be an active reader by identifying how the keywords relate to the section headers or title of the chapter."

Another way to be an active reader is to make short statements for each main point as you identify them. Here are examples of short statements regarding key points.

1. **List** the conditions, persons, or behavior/actions of the persons in the reading
2. **Define** or **describe** the conditions, persons, or behavior/actions of the persons you are reading about
3. **Identify** how the conditions or persons are similar or different
4. **Identify the causes** of the condition or person's behavior
5. **List how** the factors and/or people interact with each other
6. **List how the factors** interact and influenced the outcomes
7. **List the consequences of these interactions**

So in brief, **each paragraph has at least one main point, and each section generally has 3 to 5 main points.** As you finish a section, you should have identified at least one main thought per paragraph and three to five facts per section. Keywords should be highlighted that answer questions regarding definitions, types of conditions, causes of conditions, etc. Following this method you will find the main points and identify these main points for future reference when you are studying for the exam.

"Look for and identify 3 to 5 main points in each section of the text."

2. A second method for identifying important points is **by recognizing what your professor thinks is important by using the principle of converging operations.** The concept behind converging operations is that when an idea appears in more than one place (for example, in the text of your book, in a picture, and in the lecture) it is a strong candidate for an idea that your professor thinks is important and will be included on the next exam. Use this principle as another way to become aware of what is important in the subject you are studying.

"Important points converge – from the lecture, book and notes."

3. The third method for identifying the main thoughts is by reviewing the **learning objectives.** Learning objective are distributed by the teacher at the beginning of the course or the beginning of a new assignment. Learning objectives often state things like, "Understand the relationship between ____ and _____" or "Know the factors that increase risk for _____" or "Describe the characteristics that influence _____."
After reading the chapter and highlighting the information you find important, you should review the learning objectives for that specific chapter and go back through the chapter and find the information pertaining to each objective. Make sure you have highlighted or underlined this information, and place an asterisk (*) and a number by this information. The number means to you that this is in direct response to a specific learning objective, and this information is more likely to be information that appears on a test or quiz.

Remember, the information may be in the text, diagrams or illustrations so examine the chapter carefully until you have identified each of the facts pertaining to each learning objective.

"Find information that addresses or answers each learning objective. Place an asterisk (*) and a number by this information."

What to do if you can't find the answer to a learning objective.
Most information pertaining to the learning objectives can be found in the classroom notes and assigned readings. If however, you have difficulty locating this information, then it is time for you to become an **active learner.** Go to other resources for information such as the teacher, classmates, other textbooks and the internet. Teachers are the fastest way to find the information and the most reliable. They are also under-used by most students outside of the classroom setting.

One of the best ways to approach a teacher regarding a question is to approach them right after a lecture or during a break between lectures. Introduce yourself, if necessary, and state your question. Be prepared to write down the response provided. Have paper and pencil ready and write down the key points.

> "The instructor is a valuable resource for finding answers to questions and learning objectives. Ask them, when you can't find the answer elsewhere."

Alternatively, finding a classmate who is helpful and knowledgeable can also reduce your time searching for answers to questions and learning objectives. Just make sure you find someone who is reliable and can give reliable information. A third approach is using the internet and web-based search engines such as Google or PubMed to find additional information on the topic. Once you have acquired the answer to the learning objective, add this information to your notes or in the margin of your textbook. This way, the answer to the learning objective is readily available when you start reviewing for the exam.

> "Make sure you have addressed all the learning objectives by using reliable information resources."

3. Manage the information. **Managing information is key to a successful experience in college.** Unfortunately, many students have difficulty managing the amount of information (material) assigned during a typical college course load that amounts to about 12 to 16 credit hours. This can be even more difficult if you

don't have a study method and you are trying to compete athletically, work at a job, maintain a relationship or are living away from home for the first time. A systematic approach that allows you to condense the information works best under these circumstances.

Condense the information. After you have identified the new and important information, the next important task is to **condense the information.** This should be done at least several days before the exam, and requires condensing information from all sources including notes, assigned readings, additional readings and answers to learning objectives.

> ## "Condensing the information is important for reducing the time you need to study."

Here's how this works. About one week before the exam, take your assigned readings with the highlighted information and review the highlighted points on the page. There are likely 3 to 5 main points on each page that you should identify. Then transfer these main thoughts to a blank piece of paper. This is your **study guide.** By the time you finish a chapter that is 10 pages long you will have transferred 30 to 50 main thoughts. Be succinct. Don't write entire sentences, instead just write down the main points. Put the thoughts into lists and/or diagrams, and collate like-minded (similar) ideas. This is important since short-term memory is enhanced when similar concepts and thoughts are grouped together in "chunks of meaningful information." For example, for a history test, group together all events that occurred before the year 1800. Further, collate these events by important people, important places, or important events in which these people gathered.

> ## "Write the main points using key words in your STUDY GUIDE. Also, chunk information together so the elements are related."

Now go to your lecture notes and add to your **study guide** by putting the main points from lectures with the information on the study guide. Often you will find that the notes only reiterate the main points you wrote from the chapter. You may find a couple of new points from the notes and additional readings. Add these in the appropriate locations on your study guide.

When you are done with the chapter (including the notes and additional reading) you should have at most 1 or 2 pages of main thoughts. This is your **main study guide** from now on. Going back to the classroom notes and assigned readings shouldn't be necessary unless you need clarification of a main point that is written on your paper. (Note, if you have 5 chapters assigned for the exam, you should have only 5 to 10 pages of a **study guide** to study for the exam, so you have already condensed the information).

> **"Creating a main study guide greatly increases your efficiency. It condenses the important information, and reduces the time and amount of material you need to study."**

4. Memorize the Material. Now that you have the important information organized and recorded it a fact sheet, it is time to memorize those important facts. There are a lot of good techniques and books on how to commit things to memory. We've adapted the information described below from the very good work of Harry Lorayne and Jerry Lucas in *The Memory Book* and from techniques used by master memory champions.

Currently, it's not in vogue to teach people memory skills during the course of obtaining a formal education. It wasn't too long ago, however, that part of a good education was learning how to remember.

The fundamental memory principle is to first **simplify** the new information. This can be done using words and concepts you understand. Then, **group the new information, visualize it** and **connect it** with something you already know (remember).

> **"To memorize: simplify the new information. Group it (into a chunk of information) visualize it, and connect it with something you already know."**

Think for example of how you remember the shape of Italy. Most all of us remember the shape of Italy as a boot. Similarly, the shape of the state of Michigan resembles a glove. It's easy to remember something when you have simplified the information – in this case by **visually connecting it** to something that we already know and stored away in our minds. So, **the basic strategy for storing new information and being able to retrieve it is to: Simplify it, group it, visualize it, then connect it** *to a mental image or something that you already know.*

Let's demonstrate the technique of simplifying by grouping information. We use an anatomy lesson here.

The hand is made up of 27 bones as illustrated here. These bones are organized into three general categories that include the carpal bones, metacarpal bones, and phalanges. The carpal bones consist of the scaphoid, lunate, triquetrum, pisiform, trapezium, trapezoid, capitate, and hamate bones. The metacarpal bones appear in each finger and are numbered from I through V starting with the thumb as I and the little finger as V. There are three phalanges, the proximal, middle, and distal that are contained in every finger except for the thumb. The thumb only has a proximal and distal phalange.

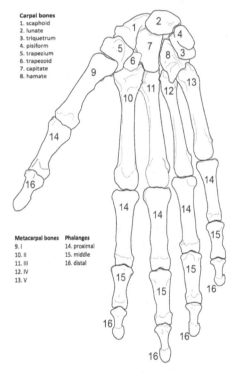

Carpal bones
1. scaphoid
2. lunate
3. triquetrum
4. pisiform
5. trapezium
6. trapezoid
7. capitate
8. hamate

Metacarpal bones
9. I
10. II
11. III
12. IV
13. V

Phalanges
14. proximal
15. middle
16. distal

While this may seem like a lot of information, let us show you how this can be simplified, by **GROUPING**. Notice on the left side of the figure, we have divided the 27 bones into 3 groups. This was not arbitrary. The mind remembers 3 connected facts better than long strings of information. This is why phone numbers are divided after the first 3 numbers to help with memory. We call this the "POWER OF 3." And, master memory champions use the power of 3 to picture the facts they are trying to memorize, often by using a string of 3 "a subject, verb and object" to commit facts to memory.

In our example, we have divided the information into three groups or categories. The 27 bones are now divided into a group of 8 carpal bones, a group of 5 metacarpal bones, and a group of 3 bones for each phalange or finger (excluding the thumb – which only has 2).

Using the "POWER of 3" all we need to memorize for the phalanges are "proximal, middle and distal." Pretty simple so far. Even easier is memorizing the metacarpal bones which are numbered one to five. They are from the knuckles to the wrist, so picture an image of your knuckles for the META-CARPAL bones. Alternatively, use "MC" to stand for metacarpal and commit to memory "**MC knuckled [the] bones**" to stand for the metacarpal bones make up your knuckles.

The third group are the CARPAL bones, also known as the bones of the wrist. These eight bones are arranged in two rows. By dividing the eight carpal bones into 2 rows of four bones each, we simplify want needs to be learned. Now, let's apply a popular technique for memorizing these CARPAL bones by using the FIRST LETTER OF EACH WORD and create a **mnemonic** – a verbal memory aid such as a poetic phrase.

A mnemonic for memorizing the CARPAL bones is "some lovers try positions that they can't handle" - the first letters of these eight words are the first letters of the names of the eight carpal bones arranged from lateral to medial, row one closest to the arm (i.e., proximal) first: scaphoid, lunate, triquitrum, pisiform/trapezium, trapezoid, capitate, hamate. So, if you spend time reciting the poetic phrase 3 times, and substitute the anatomic names for each word, you now have learned the bones of the hand.

Another way to simplify the information is by using **mental imagery**. This technique requires you to make a connection between a fact and a mental image that you can see in your mind's eye. The first step is to come up with a relationship between what you're trying to remember and what you already know by using your imagination. Then, it is important that you can see the connection in your mind as a mental picture. The ability to see the connection mentally requires that you're able to visualize or create a picture of the relationship that you can actually "see." "Picturing it" is what master memory champions use to remember a lot of information like the sequence of a deck of cards.

There are two helpful principles for creating a memorable connection that you can see as a mental image. These principles include **SUBSTITUTION** and **ACTION**.

SUBSTITUTION involves replacing a piece of the information you are trying to remember with an unusual and "pictureable" piece of information. Like the shape of Italy is a boot. The substitution can be a normal object or an EXAGGERATION where the pictured image is much bigger or out of proportion than normal scale. The exaggeration can be humorous, ridiculous (like a cartoon) or not funny at all.

The second principle is the one of action. Using the ACTION principle, you image something happening to the interconnected facts.

Let's see how you would use these principles to learn more information about the bones of the hand. Notice, that in the first row of the CARPAL bones that 'scaphoid" bone is on the thumbside and the largest. Using the techniques above you can create examples below to help you remember this information.

SUBSTITUTION: Actually, the mnemonic we just mentioned " some lovers try positions" uses word substitution for the words you need to memorize: scaphoid, lunate, triquetrum and pisiform. Alternatively you could use substitution and a mnemonic that is an EXAGGERATION "some lepricons tackle pigskins to tell coach hike" for all 8 CARPAL bones.

a. Another approach is to realize that scaphoid sounds like SCAFFOLD so you can substitute this word for scaphoid. Since a scaffold is used to hold up things like a ceiling, you can EXAGGERATE the 'picture in your mind' of the scaphoid being the biggest object in this row.

ACTION: Here you can build on your substitution of the word SCAFFOLD for scaphoid and 'picture' a scaffold holding up other things like the moon (lunate) triangle (triquetrum) and a peeing baby (pisiform). To fully apply the principle with SUBSTITUTION, EXAGGERATION AND ACTION you can picture the SCAFFOLD as being the biggest object in your mental image (since it is the biggest bone in the row) extending from the earth to the MOON with a TRIANGLE sitting on top of the moon, and a baby PEEING through the triangle.

Putting it all together, this mental image uses SUBSTITUTIONS AND ACTIONS to stand for the 1st 4 CARPAL bones in the hand. The connections are:

Scaffold-Scaphoid   Moon-Lunar   Triangle-Triquetrum   Peeing-pisiform

This mental imagery approach is outlined in greater detail in the following reference book, Lorayne, H., & Lucas, J. (1974). The Memory Book. Ballantine: New York. Use of these principles will help you develop memory connections that will enable you to remember any new piece of information for as long as you want to remember it.

5. Review periodically. We spent time in an earlier chapter talking about the importance of regular review of material as a way of building memory and learning. Remember the single most powerful technique you can use to help yourself remember information is immediate review upon original learning. Periodic review helps to ensure that information stays with you. Thus, we recommend that you plan to do periodic reviews of your **STUDY GUIDE** on a weekly basis. This method will help you consolidate the information into long-term memory storage.

6. Condense the information by identifying what you don't know. Now here is a real gem for helping you study for the approaching exam. Many of the "A" students already know this technique. That is, they take their **STUDY GUIDE** and begin quizzing themselves for information they don't know. Once they identify what they don't know – they can separate the information that needs to be learned. Thus, they have **condensed the information to be learned. We call this:**

"Identify what you don't know."

To identify the information you know from the information you don't, cover each main point with your finger or piece of paper, such as a file card. Ask yourself whether you know that point or not. Take time to learn the main point by standing up and walking around while you recite the thought. Being physically active helps. Don't try to just learn the main points while lounging in a bed or chair. Get up, recite out loud, while pressing against a firm object to work major muscle groups, or while walking back and forth (pacing). All these activities increase blood flow and the ability for your brain to learn.

"Be active while identifying what you don't know."

After reciting the main point, if still you don't know that point well or have doubts, then highlight the point and move on to the next points. Repeat this method for each point in your **STUDY GUIDE**. Review the entire page of your study guide and clearly define the material you know from that you don't know using your highlighter. After completing each page, you now have a **refined STUDY GUIDE** that highlights only the important points you don't know.

"Your refined STUDY GUIDE highlights the important points. This clearly defines what you will need to study next."

8. Study what you don't know. As the exam approaches, you should focus your efforts only on the important material you don't know – that is the high-lighted points in the refined **STUDY GUIDE**. More clearly stated, the key to this habit is to focus your efforts by "**studying what you don't know.**" **Don't waste time re-reading the chapters.** Stick to your study guide and the highlighted material.

"Study what you don't know – which daily should become less and less."

To further implement the technique, take the **highlighted points of what you don't know** that are found in your **refined STUDY GUIDE** and transfer these

Important items as the exam approaches:

- **Book and notes (use daily and weekly before the exam)**
- **Study guide (as the class starts, weekly updated)**
- **Refined study guide (reviewed 3 to 6 days before the exam)**
- **File cards (reviewed 1 to 2 days before the exam)**

points to a **FILE CARD(S)**. This allows you to take an entire page of 50+ facts and reduce them to less than 10 or 15 facts on a file card or two.

The rewriting of these points on to **FILE CARDS** accomplishes two important tasks. First, it allows you to condense the material which began as a 10 to 20 page chapter and lots of notes down to a manageable amount – 1 or 2 file cards. Second, it exposes your thinking to the topics you don't know and increases your chances of learning this material.

Do this for each chapter several days before the exam; such that you have one study guide page per chapter and one FILE CARD per chapter. The night before the exam you should review the FILE CARDS first. Make sure you know all the points on the FILE CARDS. After all, this is the information you have demonstrated you know the least. Go through each FILE CARD for each chapter. Highlight any points you don't understand or miss while quizzing yourself. Go back to the REFINED STUDY GUIDE to clarify the missed point or if needed review the assigned reading and clarify that point.

"Have the information condensed on to FILE CARDS a few days before the exam."

Don't get distracted here. Only review the point(s) in question. Sometimes it is easy to start re-reading the entire assignment. Don't do that, stay on task. Find the answer to that single point then come back to your file card and add a bit of information to clarify that point. Then go to the next **FILE CARD**. Keep the book handy as a ready resource if you need it.

Reviewing the **FILE CARDS** may only take 5 or 10 minutes per card. So, you may finish your studying the night before an exam by reviewing the 5 or so file cards in 20 minutes or less! Don't be concerned the first few times this happens, even though you may be used to spending long hours cramming the night before an exam. You need to realize that with this method of **condensing first** and **studying what you don't know**, you use much less time and are much more efficient. However, if you feel uncomfortable that you just didn't study long enough after finishing the few file cards you have, then pick up your study guide sheets and review the highlighted points, or review specific questions with a friend. Then take a break, you deserve it.

"By focusing your studying on what you don't know, you can finish studying much earlier than expected."

You should realize that based on this method, the order of importance for studying the night before the exam is the:

1st) highlighted points on the FILE CARDS,

2nd) other information on the FILE CARDS,

3rd) highlighted information in the REFINED MAIN STUDY GUIDE,

4th) other information in the STUDY GUIDE,

5th) information in the book,

6th) information in the notes, and

7th) information in the additional readings.

Now, let us be clear here. The sequence of importance listed above is based on the method we prescribe that advises you to **read the assignments, identify the main thoughts, condense the information, transfer the information to study guides and file cards, and study what you don't know.** If you follow this method, you greatly enhance your chances of academic success.

Now, doesn't that seem easy? However, we have been impressed by how often this simple concept is not applied regularly by students, especially those whose performances have been sub-par.

9. Cross the Finish Line. Another valuable skill that can improve the efficiency of your study and contribute to exam success is the ability to predict test questions. Taking a few minutes after a class to ask yourself this question, "what kind of test question could the professor ask about the material s/he just covered in class?"

Likewise, you can do the same thing with your summary pages. Get into the habit of **predicting test questions** you're likely to see on an upcoming quiz or exam. Once you have developed a series of questions that you might be expecting, **practice answering those questions just like you would for a test.** In fact, we would encourage you to answer those questions under some time pressure, so that you experience what it's like to work with the material under such pressure. For example, take about 15 minutes to answer 10 to 12 questions.

Research studies on learning have shown that the conditions under which you first learn information are likely the conditions under which you will remember that information best. To take advantage of this finding, use time pressure during your study time to help you do your best on an exam - when you'll also have time pressure.

"Practice by answering questions under some time pressure."

Good students study to learn with the intent to do their best on exams. You need to be able to focus your time in effective ways, so please remember that you want to be careful spending time with material that you already know. Focus on information that you don't know and need to commit to memory.

Backward Planning Means Planning Ahead. In all of our time as both students and professors we have yet to find that significant EXAMS just pop up on the schedule unexpectedly. Generally there is considerable advanced warning of an upcoming EXAM. This gives you an opportunity to plan whether or not you want to be successful. If you want to do your best, you must have the discipline to set aside time regularly for study. You also need to be able to do backward planning that we will discuss in the next section.

Discipline. The word, "**discipline**", usually brings up a variety of negative memories in students. It is hardly ever used to reflect positive attributes especially as we are growing up. Discipline is, however, an important key to successful study habits. For you see, discipline really means **staying focused on your goals.** That's why your goals are the foundation of this entire approach to being a successful student. It is discipline that enables you to set aside time to study and remain faithful to following through. Use your schedule or calendar to plan study activities ahead of time.

"Be disciplined in your study habits."

Backward planning. Backward planning is simply working backwards from the deadline or due date for a project or task. Determine how much time you need to read a chapter, prepare your notes, read your notes, and take into account those things necessary to prepare yourself for an exam. If one chapter takes one hour to read, and you have five chapters, then you're going to need to plan at least five hours of study time to complete the reading. We encourage you to set aside the time you will need to prepare yourself adequately. Generally, this is over several (at least three) days in advance of the exam date. You need to create for yourself reasonable scenarios for the amount of time it will take for you to be ready to do your best on an exam.

"Plan reasonable amount of study time in advance of the exam."

How much time is the right amount of time? This is a question that is based on the individual learning rate of each student, but generally requires about 2 hours for every lecture hour. In order to have the time to put together a comprehensive study strategy, you **need to measure the volume of material and make decisions about which parts of the material you know and don't know.** There is a difference between knowing the material and being familiar with the material. Doing your best on an exam requires the confidence that comes when you know that you know the material.

Summary Habit 4:

- Use the planning suggestions, study techniques and memorization skills outlined here to prepare properly for your exams.

- Remember, if you have a schedule, you are less likely to procrastinate – and therefore less likely to become overwhelmed.

Demonstrate your abilities: Test taking skills.

In this chapter you will learn the importance of:

1) Pre-exam strategies
2) Day of exam strategies
3) Post-exam strategies

It was a very hot August afternoon with two soccer teams battling hard for a victory. One team was drinking mostly ice water; the other team was drinking mostly a popular sports drink. Not surprisingly, the team with access to the sports drink used almost twice the volume of fluids during the game as the other team. So, who ultimately won the game? In the second half the team using the sports drink looked stronger, ran faster, and overall appeared to play harder for each ball. The game ended with the score 2-1 in favor of the team using the sports drink. When it comes time to demonstrate your abilities, those who know how to take full advantage of the resources available to them will most likely reap the rewards of success.

We'd like to begin this chapter with some general comments. First of all, if you don't prepare and study for an exam and don't know the material, it's unlikely that you will do well or even pass the exam. The information in this chapter is not going to replace knowledge and careful preparation for an exam. We do hope, however, that the information provided in this text will help you do your best and avoid common errors when you take exams. You should never rely on exam techniques alone to pass, but having a set of test taking skills should improve your performance and enhance your confidence when taking an exam. There are no special tricks or gimmicks that we'll be discussing, but rather we will be dealing with basic principles and the application of those principles to the task of taking a test.

1. Pre-exam strategies - Spaced Practice. The amount of time needed to perform well (i.e., length of your study periods) is based on the amount of material on the exam. For example, one chapter may only require one night of study, whereas 4 or more chapters will likely require four nights of study. As a guideline, you should set aside the same number of nights studying in advance of the exam as the number of chapters to be tested, and twice the number of lecture hours to be covered on the exam.

> ## "Set aside the same number of nights to study as the number of chapters that will be on the exam."

The first exam-taking strategy is to remember that spaced practice is one of the keys to success. You can't do your best if you don't have the time to prepare and space your preparations over a reasonable period of time. An essential part of spaced practice is to set aside time for reading the assignments, reviewing your STUDY GUIDE and practicing answering simulated test questions under conditions that closely resemble those that will be prevailing during the actual test.

> ## "Space your study times (i.e., practice sessions) over a reasonable period of time that allows you to focus on your STUDY GUIDE a day or two before the exam."

For eample, set aside 45 minutes one or two days in advance of the exam and write down twenty possible test questions. DO THIS UNDER TIME PRESSURE. Use this time to answer the questions without looking at your notes, text or study guide. Then check your answers by reviewing your notes, text and study guide. Circle or highlight the questions you missed, and add these facts to your STUDY GUIDE. This will mentally prepare you for the exam, strengthen your study guide, and reinforce information that you have learned.

> ## "Take a practice exam a couple days in advance of the exam."

Self-Care. The second pre-exam strategy is to make sure you take care of yourself physically. This means regular sleep, regular physical activity, and a nutrition program that will have your mind and body working at its best. Since mental activity requires an adequate level of glucose as the brain's primary energy source, it's wise to have a nutritional strategy that will ensure that glucose levels in the blood are maintained while you're taking the exam. This means that it's helpful to think and act like a long-distance runner, or other athlete, who is preparing for a big challenge or race that will require endurance. Athletes know that good nutrition, particularly the day before the athletic event is critical. We encourage you to eat healthily, particularly the day before the exam, so that you have an adequate supply of complex carbohydrates and proteins to fuel your body.

Your diet leading up to the exam. As a general rule, you should provide your brain with regular meals and a balanced diet. Foods rich in omega-3 fatty acids (fish, dark leafy greens, nuts and olive oil) are recommended, because these foods are thought to increase your ability to concentrate, learn and memorize facts. You should consume at least 2 to 4 ounces (30- 75 grams of protein) of fish or meat per day and eat this with low glycemic index foods (beans, whole grain breads, oats, pasta, fruit and vegetables). These foods are more slowly absorbed by the blood than high glycemic foods (i.e., candy snacks) and help to maintain more constant blood glucose levels. When dining, drink plenty of fluids (16 ounces per meal). Brain power is optimized by proper hydration and benefits from the presence of antioxidants. So, eat lots of fruits and vegetables.

"Brain power is fueled by proper nutrition and hydration."

On the day of the exam, make sure you eat breakfast and plan your nutritional intake in accordance with when you take the exam. You want to have a nutritional strategy that ensures your blood glucose levels are maintained, and that sufficient fuel is available from a meal at the time of the exam. Otherwise, stored energy is mobilized to feed your brain. To allow your brain to function most efficiently, you should eat a meal about 1 to 2 hours before an exam so the nutrients are delivered to the brain at the time you need for your brain to work.

"Feed your brain the night before and the day of an exam."

Example of brain food before an exam:
Breakfast (1 to 2 hours before the exam)

- Eggs (e.g., Western [or spinach] omelet), plus whole grain bread toast and 16 ounces of orange juice
  -Eggs are rich in choline which is used to help transmit nerve impulses
  -Vegetables in the omelet are rich in antioxidants.
  -Whole grain breads are enriched with vitamin B

Avoid the following:
- Skipping a meal (or fast) before an exam
- Eating a huge meal right before an exam
- Eating junk food before an exam
- Eating a diet high in saturated and trans fats (i.e., cakes, cookies, processed desserts, chips, fatty dairy products, fatty cuts of meat)
- Consuming alcohol before an exam

"Be smart about your nutrition and you will perform smartly on your exams."

This pre-exam strategy is advantageous because it 1) prepares you mentally for the exam by providing spaced practice, and 2) provides your body a steady supply of glucose to fuel your brain during studying and the exam.

2. Day of the Exam Strategies. On the day of the exam, plan on arriving at the examination room several minutes early and plan in advance for potential delays (e.g., traffic, accidents, adverse weather conditions – like rain or snow, and unexpected conversations). Few things can be more upsetting than showing up late for an exam. Also, it is generally not a good idea to compare your test preparation with others. You should be focusing on the task at hand and deliberately avoid listening to the conversations of others about their exam preparation. Right before an exam, listening to others talk about their test preparation could create questions in your own mind about your preparation for the exam and weaken your own mental set. **Confidence and focus are important dimensions of good exam performance.** You don't want to undermine either of these factors by listening to the comments of others right before exam. Be confident of your preparation and don't worry how others have prepared.

> ## "Arrive early, be confident and focused. Also, avoid comparing exam study strategies with others."

Exam Taking Strategies. At the beginning of this discussion, we want to emphasize how important it is to do your own work. The sense of self-confidence knowing that you have done your best and you haven't cheated yourself will set a pattern for lifetime success. Character is what you do when no one else is looking. We're writing this book to give you the skills to do your best and take advantage of the opportunity to learn. Knowledge is a gift to be cherished and nurtured. We're not writing this book for you to be taking shortcuts to receive a grade, but rather, to help you learn how to work smart so that you can accomplish the life goals you set for yourself as you build your mind's capacity to think and create. It is important to point out that learning matters and how you demonstrate it is key in making your mark in life. Don't begin to erode the opportunity to make a difference in your life by cheating on a test. Choose to do the right thing; start by doing your own work on an exam.

> ## "Do your own work on the exam."

Okay, so we've gotten the parental thing out of the way. Now, the first thing to focus on when you get your exam is to review the exam from the beginning to the end. Make sure that you have all the items that were supposed to be included on the exam. In addition to insuring that you have a complete exam and knowing where all the items are, this survey will enable you to develop a plan for managing your time.

"Survey the exam to estimate how much time you should spend on each question."

Available time. You should use all the time available for the exam. The students first done with an exam generally don't get the best scores; remind yourself of that when you see students getting finished with the exam halfway through the exam period. Plan to use all the time that's available to you and make sure you don't spend too much time on any one question. That's one of the reasons why you want to complete a general survey of the number and types of questions on the exam, right at the start. This survey will allow you to know approximately how much time to spend with each question.

"Don't rush through an exam; use all the time given to you."

Difficult questions and marking on the exam. If you get hung up on a question, mark it in some way (e.g., circle the question) and move on. Sometimes there will be other information in the exam that will help you with that question. Speaking of marking on your test, always take advantage of this option and use the test itself to help organize your thoughts and develop your answers. Write on your test as much as you need to (even though some instructors may say not to). Use the test itself as a document to help you think through the answers, write out thoughts, and calculate numbers. Finally, if you are using an answer sheet for electronic grading make sure that you answer every question, and there are no stray marks on the answer sheet that could interfere with electronic grading.

"Write on your test as much as you need to."

One of the advantages of using all the time available for an exam is that you should double check your answers and for any marking errors. Especially on multiple-choice tests, you want to take a few minutes to ensure that every answer you have chosen is coded correctly on to the answers sheet. As you are wrapping up, you should routinely go through the test, starting with the last item and work your way to the first item to ensure that the answers you have selected are properly coded on the answer sheet. Going in reverse (from the last question to the beginning) is an important technique that more accurately catches mistakes, because your eye is not accustomed to this order. We have found, as instructors of many thousands of students, unfortunately there is often a student who comes with a lament that they mistakenly coded their answer sheet. So, make a vow to always double check your work. That way you always get credit for what you know.

> ## "After completing the test, double check your answers recorded on your answer sheet starting with the last question going forward."

Be true to yourself. One of the major challenges associated with taking an exam, particularly a multiple-choice exam is making sure you don't lie to yourself. How do you lie to yourself? The most common way is to tell yourself that you know something, when you really don't. One of the best ways to protect from lying to yourself, is by self-talk (i.e., having an internal conversation with yourself). Self-talking is fast and it allows you to explain your thoughts so you can determine if your choice is correct. I can remember many times during an exam when I thought I knew what the answer was, but I really didn't. If you take the time to tell yourself what the answer should be, you will find it is much more difficult to assume you know what the correct answer is.

> ## "Use self-talk to ensure your answers are correct."

Changing answers. This leads to a general comment about the common saying, "never change an answer." Actually, the proper utterance should be "never change a correct answer"; however, "you can change a guess" and "don't hesitate to change a wrong answer." Sometimes guessing takes advantage of recognition memory where you match information, but you don't know the basis for that match. When you truly don't know the answer to a question, so long as there are no penalties for guessing, go ahead and guess. But when you go back to reviewing the exam before you turn it in, don't change a guess, unless it is a wrong answer. How do you know, if it's a wrong answer? If you can tell yourself internally or quietly out loud, what the reason is for changing your guess, then do so. If no clear reason be can be stated to yourself, leave the guess on your answer sheet.

"Don't change an answer, unless you can state the exact reason for changing the answer."

True or false questions. Now we'd like to talk about taking specific kinds of tests. The first type of test is the true / false test. For a true / false test, there are usually three parts: a fact, a second fact, and a relationship between the two facts. Your job is to determine if either fact is false, or if the relationship is false, because if anything is false, then the answer is false. Remember, **if you find one exception to any part of a statement in a true or false question, the question is false.** Look for, circle or underline the keywords in the statement to help you identify the main facts in the relationship. Also, find specific words that describe inclusive relationships, like 'always', 'never', and 'every' that make the relationship more restrictive. If you find one exception then the item is false.

Underline the keywords in the statement to help determine if the entire statement is true.

Example:

True or False   Abraham Lincoln was the 15th president of the United States.

The keywords are: Abraham Lincoln   15th   president
                        United States

Of these keywords, "15th" is the main keyword because the obvious is that he was a president, however the discriminatory factor is whether he was the 14th, 15th or 16th president. We suggest circling 15th as the question is either true or false based on this adjective. If you studied and learned your history, you will remember he was the 16th president and realize that this statement is false. However, it **illustrates that one word in the question often is the keyword for determining the correct answer.** It is your job to find the most important keyword in each question and circle it. This method will help you answer these types of questions correctly.

Matching. When you're faced with a test that requires matching, link all those items that you know, first. Then the task is significantly reduced if there may be items that you don't know. Don't get stuck with the first item when you don't know the answer. Skip over the unknowns and proceed to match up all the items that you do know. Then come back and complete the matches of the remaining unknowns. This way you get credit for what you know and for being smart about using the process of elimination.

"Match what you know first, then complete matches of the remaining items."

Multiple choice questions. For multiple-choice items, your basic approach should be to "reason rather than recognize." The first point in taking multiple-choice questions is to read all the items. Be very careful to pick an answer until you have read every item. Also, don't go looking for an answer that you think should be there[*].

[*]Looking for a pre-conceived answer when it does not appear in the list of choices is a source of frustration for many students. You need to realize that although you may want to look for the answer that you have pre-programmed your brain to be correct – your answer may not appear amongst the choices. This is because teachers have more than one way of listing "the best" answer. You need to realize that teachers may not put your choice as an option, and you have to choose from the teacher's choices. So avoid this frustration, and instead read each multiple choice offered and select the best from the 4 or 5 choices presented. Remember the answer doesn't have to be your answer, it only needs to be better than all the other choices listed.

"With multiple choice questions, the correct answer is often just better than the other choices listed. Look for the best answer, not necessarily the exact response you had in mind."

Secondly, eliminate the obvious wrong answers by "crossing them out or strike through them," thus limiting your choices. Then, select the best answer from the remaining alternatives.

In the case where you have no idea about what the correct answer is, try to eliminate one choice then circle this question so you can come back to it at the end of the exam, then move on to the next question. Return to the circled item after you have answered all other questions in the test. Then, eliminate the obvious, use other information found in the test, **and try to end up with two answers that are similar.** One of the goals of good test construction is to create just this scenario, where the correct answer is one of two similar appearing items. So when you have no idea how to correctly answer a question, look for two similar items and ask yourself what makes them different? This approach helps to locate the correct answer.

Test Questions Have one...

a. Best answer
b. correct, But not Best
c. One partly correct
d. Incorrect answer

Another strategy when guessing is to beware of long item responses. Sometimes, long items are put in to distract you, but there are occasions where professors with poor test construction skills will put a long answer in the test that is correct. Be on your guard when you see an obviously long answer.

Remember to perform at your best. Guard against careless recording errors, reason rather than guess, and take the time to review your test when you're finished. Multiple choice test taking is a skill that can be learned. So, get credit for what you know by not being intimidated by having to take these types of exams.

Essay questions. For essay test questions, it's important to scan the entire series of questions first so that you get an idea of how to plan the sequence in which you'll answer the questions. Note the point values associated with each test item so you can apportion your time accordingly. You don't want to waste a lot of time with low point value items and leave high point value items unaddressed.

"Survey the questions and know the point values assigned to each question."

Once you've decided the order with which you will respond, for the first question briefly sketch an outline of the main points and keywords you will use in your proposed answer. Organize yourself by arranging the keywords in the sequence they will appear in your answer. Decide on the number of paragraphs you will use based on the main points you wish to make, then include a summary paragraph at the very end. When you write, use good grammatical construction.

> ## "List and arrange main points and keywords in an outline prior to writing your essay. This will help you decide on the number of paragraphs you will be writing."

Remember the formula for a good paragraph (introductory sentence, supporting sentences, and closing sentence that links the paragraph to the one that will follow). Take the time to write neatly. Most often you will write an essay with a pencil, as this allows for you correct thoughts and sentences as you go. However, there are occasions where you may want to use pen for your answer. If you take the time to sketch your answer in rough draft form, then the use of pen for your final answer is a way to communicate powerfully to your professor or teacher your level of learning and confidence.

> ## "A good paragraph is composed of 4 or 5 sentences, is organized and conveys main points in a logical manner."

You should use examples in your answers so that phrases like "for instance," "for example", "as illustrated by", and "in the case of" are sprinkled liberally throughout your response. Cite authorities other than yourself in your answers, and be accurate in attributing the correct authority with the point being made.

> ## "Citing examples and authorities demonstrates your knowledge of the topic."

Finally, take all the allotted time you are given for the exam, and reread your answers to ensure they make sense. Using all the time allotted allows you to reread your responses, refine your essay that results in a strong, logical position.

> ## "Use your time to reread, refine and ensure your essay is a logical response to the question."

3. Post exam strategies. Most students breathe a sigh of relief after an exam and go on to other things quickly. The life of a student is constantly moving on and what matters is the final score on the exam. Don't fall into this habit. Use the exam as a learning tool and take advantage of an opportunity to visit with your professor to review your exam. This will help the professor put a face with your name, you can learn how s/he thinks and develops an exam (this will come in handy for predicting future test questions), and you can learn from your mistakes. Ask the professor for help in learning to master the material in the course. Your goal should be to use the test experience as an opportunity to further your understanding of the material.

> ## "Use the test to increase your understanding of the material. Be a lifelong learner."

Contesting answers to test questions. There may be occasions where you find that the test question was not well constructed or there may be more than one correct answer. In these circumstances, you should inquire of the course policy for handling contested test questions. In college courses, there may be a student committee that handles these questions. You should submit your question to this committee, and the committee brings the contested questions to the instructor for review.

In other instances, it will be up to you to bring the "question in question" to the attention of the course instructor. Your concern should be voiced as soon as possible after the exam. A good approach is to ask the instructor during the exam review or during his/her office hours. Be polite and non-confrontational. Read the question and what you think is a good alternative answer. Refer to the textbook or class notes to support your position. Generally, alternative answers that have good support will be accepted by the instructor, especially if you are not confrontational or demeaning.

> ## "Use accurate sources to support your position when contesting an answer to a test question."

Summary Habit 5:

- Prepare for exams with a game plan that includes pre-exam strategies (spaced practice and self care), day of exam strategies (test taking skills and time management), and post-exam strategies (learning from tests).

- It is important that you demonstrate what you know to yourself and to others.

Putting it all together:
Live your life with purpose.

In this chapter you will learn the importance of:

1) Enjoying the journey
2) Doing your best
3) Maintaining the balance
4) Helping yourself while helping others

We have been describing a comprehensive method to help you do your best and work efficiently because we're committed to empowering you with the tools to learn. Learning is an important key to life success, but one of your greatest challenges to learning will be managing your time and energy as you face many competing demands for your time.

So, it is logical for you to ask, "How do I decide what's important and how do I spend my time?'"

The answer to these two questions relies on having two goals at the same time. The goals are to: **(1) enjoy what you are doing and (2) work to do your best.** These goals are a paradox and generally create tension with which it is good for you to wrestle. Deciding how to spend your time and energy requires that you learn to balance your life.

Remember, life is too short to be miserable and there needs to be time for rest and play, as well as for hard work. Believe us that there is plenty of hard work required for success, but you can learn to be efficient in how you do that work. Your goal should be to learn how to have positive emotions a majority of your waking hours in all that you do.

"Life is too short to be miserable...enjoy what you are doing and work to do your best."

Good decisions come when your mind is in a positive, relaxed state. Experiencing positive feelings should not depend on your circumstances because you have a choice in how you feel regardless of life events that come your way. Learn how to focus on what is good and positive (deliberately remind yourself of things that you are thankful for) in the present moment rather than on disappointments, frustrations, or unexpected obstacles that can weigh you down. Of course, there are times to mourn, be angry, or feel disappointment, but such times should be worked through so that you can move on and again experience positive, relaxed feelings necessary for you to work at your best.

"Be positive – you have a choice in how you feel."

Maintaining a positive emotional state in difficult circumstances requires courage and deliberate investment in the three "C's" of the hardy person. The first "C" stands for Commitment to the importance of what you are doing so that you stay the course and keep involved with activities and people in your life regardless of what comes your way.

The second "C" represents the Challenges – those stressors in your life that help you grow as you learn from disruptions, failures and unexpected events that come your way. Too often, we believe that an easy, comfortable life is what would be best for us, but that is often not the case and it is important to find meaning and purpose in all that we encounter because we have an opportunity to grow, learn, and test ourselves with these challenges.

The third "C" is Control or the belief that regardless of what may be happening you can control certain things that allow you to make a difference by what you are doing and accomplishing. To take control, you should try to influence outcomes rather than sit by and let things happen or hope for the return of the "good old days" of your past. Commitment, challenge, and control are the hallmarks of a person who faces life events head on and uses them to grow and learn. Take advantage of this knowledge about the hardy person, and deliberately work on cultivating the three "C's" in your own life.

Invest in the 3 C's
Commitment, Challenges and Control
to help stay positive.

You have a choice in how you feel, so don't let yourself dwell on negative moods. Develop the capacity to be an optimist in life. Look for opportunities to be grateful for what you have. Learn how to resolve differences with others (through communication, negotiation and discussion); apologize when you've made a mistake or were wrong.

Take responsibility for your actions, and build relationships with kind words and deeds. Building relationships is a key task for life success, particularly when you find yourself in difficult situations. As you develop a network of satisfying relationships, you create opportunities to learn important life skills, particularly the skill of controlling how you feel. You can capture and hold feelings of a quiet, relaxed state of mind that is experiencing joy and seeking insights that will enable you to make really good decisions and problem solve with great creativity. Each of us can remember a time in our lives when we made a good decision. Those positive feelings that accompanied a good decision can be cultivated and sustained so that you can regularly be an excellent problem solver and creative thinker. Creative thinking and insights are incubated in a positive, relaxed state of mind that is open to questions and answers. Sure, it's a lifelong challenge to develop such skills, but it's well worth it and your contributions will be notable!

"Incubate your creative thinking by surrounding yourself with a positive relaxed mind."

Recent research points to the value of a pleasant mood and being engaged in doing meaningful work as important keys to happiness. Learning is about being able to contribute to the betterment of society, not just personal success. It's about giving back by making the world a better place moment by moment as you faithfully exercise your talents and gifts. Mother Theresa was said to have a card on her desk with the words, "Faithfulness not success." While personal success may be a by-product of your education and learning, you will leave a stronger legacy if you contribute towards making things better. Dream big and give yourself to big causes. Margaret Mead noted, "Never doubt that a small group of dedicated individuals can change the world. In fact, it is the only thing that ever has."

"Contribute towards making things better."

Your spiritual life also must be nurtured in the learning process. Find a purpose for your life and live out that purpose. Rick Warren in his best-selling book, The Purpose Driven Life, describes the importance of recognizing what you are made for and to do. Take advantage of the wisdom found in spiritual writings like the Pentateuch, Talmud, Koran, or Holy Bible as well as spiritual leaders, teachers and mentors to help you develop a foundation for answering the question of what your purpose in life is. You may develop many answers to this single question as you age, and each answer will help shape your decisions and actions that ultimately provide the compass bearings for your life choices.

"Find your purpose in life from the wisdom of others."

Do your best (spend the best part of your day and your energies on learning) in all that you do. Determine to become an expert in some area, not just someone who is better than most, or all of the people in your class. An expert is defined as someone who performs, on average, at a very high level. Each time you do something, do it well and in a manner that helps others. In that way, you will become the kind of person who will make a difference in whatever you choose to do. Becoming an expert starts by laying the foundation of a broad education and teaching yourself to become open-minded and an expert learner. That is one of the reasons we wrote this book.

"Finding your purpose in life will keep you striving to do good and be an expert at what you do."

Summary: Our bottom line here is to balance enjoying what you're doing and doing your best. Hold both of these principles close to you, because working on these two ideas will help you stay balanced. We caution you to not over invest in one of these activities at the expense of the other. Imbalance between enjoying and doing your best can limit your capacity to make a difference. Work to balance these two principles in your life and you'll invest your time wisely.

"Find the balance in your life, so your knowledge and expertise helps others and you take delight in these activities along your way."

References

1. Newport C. How to Become a Straight A Student. Broadway Books, New York, NY.

2. Newport C. How to Win at College. Broadway Books, New York, NY.

3. How People Learn: Brain, Mind, Experience, and School. National Research Council. National Academy Press, Washington, D.C.

4. Robinson, A. What Smart Students Know. Random House, 1993, New York, NY.

5. How to Get A's in College. Northcutt F. ed., Hundreds of Heads Books. 2007, Atlanta, GA.

6. College Unzipped: An All-Access, Backstage Pass into College Life. Kaplan Publishing, 2007, New York, NY.

7. Jensen, E. Student Success Secrets, 5th ed. Barron's Educational Series, Inc., 2003, Hauppauge, NY.

8. Ten Habits of Successful Students, excerpted from Kirszner and Mandell, The Brief Handbook, 4th ed. Cengage Learning, Florence, KY.

9. Covey S. The Seven Habits of Highly Effective Teens. Fireside; Simon & Schuster, 1998, New York, NY.

10. Kornhauser AW. How to Study: Suggestions for High School & College Students, 3rd ed. The University of Chicago Press, 1993, Chicago, IL.

11. Edutopia website at: http://www.edutopia.org/

12. http://www.ted.com/

Habit 1: Target what you want

Checklist

(Check each box when complete)

[ ] I understand that education is an important investment.

[ ] I am motivated to learn.

[ ] I have established my goals for academic achievement.

[ ] I have academic goals for this semester.

[ ] I have academic goals for this year.

[ ] I have academic goals for all 4 years of my schooling.

[ ] I understand that I will be prepared for class, read the assignments and study well in advance of the exams.

[ ] I am investing my time, mind and money in my education.

Habit 1: Target what you want

My goals for this semester are: _____
_____
_____

Course 1: _____

Course 2: _____

Course 3: _____

Course 4: _____

Course 5: _____

My goals for employment are: _____
_____
_____
_____

[ ] I understand that achieving these goals will require hard work.

Why it works: When I set goals, my life has direction.

Habit 2: Grasp new information

Checklist

(Check each box when complete)

[ ] I read, recite and review course information.

[ ] I read assignments before class.

[ ] I read in designated 30 minute blocks.

[ ] I am being time efficient.

[ ] I highlight information in the book.

[ ] I write down questions as I read and review.

[ ] I use key words to help memorize.

[ ] I attend class and take notes during class.

[ ] I review my notes and use key words to help memorize.

[ ] I have visited with my course instructors.

Habit 2: Grasp new information

I plan on reading course materials the following days and times:

_____

_____

_____

_____

_____

I plan on studying the following days and times:

_____

_____

_____

_____

I plan on meeting my course instructors on the following days:

_____

_____

_____

_____

_____

Why it works: When I study, I learn. Sharing time with my instructors allows me to receive advice for success.

Habit 3: Organize yourself

Checklist

(Check each box when complete)

[ ] I am organized. My course materials are in folders/binders.

[ ] I have the required books for each course.

[ ] I have read the course syllabus and understand classroom expectations.

[ ] I manage my time well and use a calendar of events.

[ ] Daily I write down a list of things I should do.

[ ] I study in an environment that helps me learn.

[ ] I study regularly.

[ ] I plan ahead: I know when my assignments are due, and when quizzes and exams are scheduled.

[ ] I exercise, eat a nutritious diet and get enough sleep.

Habit 3: Organize yourself

Evidence that I am organized is found in the list below.

_____

_____

_____

_____

I have ____ quizzes this semester:

I have ____ exams this semester:

The dates of my quizzes are:

_____

The dates of my exams are: _____

_____

_____

I am staying healthy. I exercise ____ days / week; typically at ____ (am/pm).

Why it works: The prepared and organized student is proactive, and ready for learning.

Habit 3: Organize yourself

My to do list

To do today:

1. _____

2. _____

3. _____

4. _____

5. _____

To do today:

1. _____

2. _____

3. _____

4. _____

5. _____

Habit 3: Organize yourself

My to do list

To do today:

1. _____

2. _____

3. _____

4. _____

5. _____

To do today:

1. _____

2. _____

3. _____

4. _____

5. _____

Habit 4: Prepare for exams

Checklist

(Check each box when complete)

[ ] I plan and prepare each day.

[ ] I create a MASTER SCHEDULE showing all exam dates.

[ ] I evaluate the amount of materials to be on the exam and provide at least two hours of studying per lecture hour covered per exam.

[ ] I read the chapters well in advance of the exam.

[ ] I identify the important material from books and my notes and highlight the important facts.

[ ] I condense the important information and build a STUDY GUIDE.

[ ] I use my study guide to review regularly and memorize.

[ ] I identify what I don't know and ask the instructor or tutors to learn what I don't know.

[ ] I predict test questions in advance to clarify what I don't know.

[ ] I use the day before the exam to study what I don't know, then review what I already know.

Habit 4: Prepare for exams

Example of a Study Guide

List the conditions, persons, behavior/actions of key persons or events: _____
_____
_____
_____

Why is this event important? _____
_____
_____

List interacting factors and connections: _____
_____
_____

List how the factors interact and influence the outcomes:
_____
_____

List the consequence of key person/event actions and interactions:
_____
_____
_____

Why it works: A study guide allows you to condense the important information. Using a guide saves time and makes learning easier.

Habit 5: Demonstrate your abilities

Checklist

(Check each box when complete)

[ ] I implement pre-exam strategies. For example, I set aside the same number of nights to study as the number of chapters that will be covered on the exam.

[ ] I space my study time over several days.

[ ] I take a pretest and circle / highlight questions I miss.

[ ] I eat nutritiously the days before an exam and the day of the exam.

[ ] I get at least 6 hours of sleep the night before the exam.

[ ] On exam day, I arrive early; I am relaxed, prepared, confident and focused.

[ ] I survey the exam and know the point values assigned.

[ ] I don't rush through an exam. I use all the time provided.

[ ] I identify key words and write down thoughts as needed.

[ ] I use all the time provided and double check my answers.

[ ] I learn from tests and use the information to do well in the future.

Habit 5: Demonstrate your abilities

Your test scores are more likely to increase if you review your exam performance. I reviewed the following exams with my professors (course, grade and date):

_____ (date)	_____ (date)
_____ (date)	_____ (date)
_____ (date)	_____ (date)
_____ (date)	_____ (date)
_____ (date)	_____ (date)
_____ (date)	_____ (date)
_____ (date)	_____ (date)

Evaluate your performing after each exam. If you are not performing to best of your ability and your grades are below your target, you should discuss your performance with an instructor or counselor, or obtain a tutor. My personal plan of action is:

_____

_____

_____

_____

_____

_____

_____

_____

_____

_____

Why it works: Evaluating your performance helps you stay on target. Identifying corrective action early is key to doing well.

Habit 6: Putting it all together

Checklist

(Check each box when complete)

[ ] I am doing my best in each of my classes.

[ ] I am maintaining balance.

[ ] I am enjoying each day.

[ ] I relaxed my mind today.

[ ] I am positive and help others as I go.

[ ] I learn each day.

Habit 6: Putting it all together

I realize learning is an important key to life success. Things I learned today: _____

_____

_____

_____

_____

I am committed to doing: _____

_____

_____

_____

I am challenged by: _____

_____

_____

_____

I will take control of my challenge(s) by: _____

_____

_____

_____

Why it works: Being positive is your choice. Being positive helps you and others learn. Educated persons are more relaxed, informed and capable of finding appropriate solutions to problems.

Notes:

Examples of how I am making a difference: _____

_____

_____

_____

_____

_____

_____

_____

_____

_____

Examples of how I am helping others and society: _____

_____

_____

_____

_____

_____

_____

_____

_____

_____

_____

_____

Notes:

_____

_____

_____

_____

_____

_____

_____

_____

_____

_____

_____

_____

_____

_____

_____

_____

_____

_____

_____

_____

_____

_____

_____

_____

_____

Notes:

About the Authors

Charley Carlson, Ph.D. and Craig Miller, D.M.D., M.S., both Professors at the University of Kentucky, are academic leaders whose interest in helping students of all ages learn how to succeed academically led to this book. They have over 50 combined years in academia and in providing instruction, knowledge and learning methods to students at all phases of their lives and academic careers. Dr. Carlson is a board certified clinical psychologist who teaches developmental psychology and Dr. Miller is a clinician and expert in diagnostic sciences. In this book they emphasize the importance of a simple and step-wise approach to learning as well as the use of performance techniques that lead to academic success. Together the authors provide a unique perspective of the learning process in today's fast paced world. Their motivation for this book is to share information that leads to academic successes and is based on personal observations and research into the successes and failures of student achievements. The authors hope this book not only helps the reader, but helps the many people who will come in contact with the reader later in life. In turn, a percentage of the proceeds from the sale of these books will be donated to the American Cancer Society, so the reader's interest in learning will benefit others directly.

CPSIA information can be obtained
at www.ICGtesting.com
Printed in the USA
LVHW04s2328130618
580716LV00007B/14/P